THE RESEARCH PROJECT BOOK

by
Nancy Polette

Additional Activities by Mavis Arizzi

Cover Illustration by Marsha Baker

Copyright © 1986 by Nancy Polette

ISBN 0-913839-51-5

Book Lures Inc.

P.O. Box 9450
O'Fallon, Mo.
63366

Printed in U.S.A.

THE RESEARCH PROJECT BOOK

CONTENTS

The Research Project Book

by

Nancy Polette

INTRODUCTION

By about grade four, students in schools with library/media programs have, for the most part, achieved familiarity with the contents of their particular media center and have acquired most of the basic skills of location of library/media materials. It would follow then that by the end of grade four that independent study projects should be a basic part of the curriculum. However, regardless of the skills the student may possess, many research assignments do not call for the utilization of these skills. Teachers bemoan the fact that most students tend to copy information from the encyclopedia or the handiest reference book and that the majority of research assignments are not looked forward to eagerly by students.

In traveling throughout the United States and Canada and in interviewing several hundred teachers a year it is this writer's guess that sixty to seventy percent of research projects carried out by students are at the KNOWLEDGE or copying level. These same teachers who have been interviewed show both a willingness and a desire to move students from this initial copy stage to research projects which require analysis and synthesis of data as well as problem-solving and evaluation.

The key to moving students from lower to higher levels of thinking in the research activity is PRODUCT. If we change the product we change the process the student uses to obtain the product. For example, if the student is asked to do a report on a particular state, the typical response is to copy several paragraphs about that state from the encyclopedia. The thinking level used is KNOWLEDGE. When we change the product we also change the thinking level required. The assignment might be as follows: The White House has called and your family has been selected as the typical family for your state. The President is coming to dinner. Plan a menu. You may serve only those things raised or grown in your state. You may use only ingredients raised or grown in your state.

With the foregoing assignment the student must first locate the information. Second, he or she must analyze the information in order to combine separate elements in a new way (synthesis) to create a menu. Thus the higher levels of thinking are achieved through the changing of the research product.

Many teachers use picture books as patterns for creative writing. Non-fiction books can be used in the same way as patterns for those kinds of research projects which require not only the use of the skills of location and acquisition, but the development of divergent products based on the pattern in a particular book. Several examples follow.

BOOKS TO INTRODUCE THE VOCABULARY OF A TOPIC

Jane Howard's WHEN I'M SLEEPY (Dutton 1985) shows a little girl sleeping with a variety of animals. She is in a den with a bear, a nest with a bird and is shown in both the position and habitat of the animal. Young researchers might report on animal habits with books entitled WHEN I'M HUNGRY or WHEN I WANT TO PLAY. Their books would follow this pattern by showing or describing animals eating or at play.

THE ROSE IN MY GARDEN (Greenwillow 1984) by Arnold Lobel introduces flowering plants. Each page introduces a new plant and shows its location in relation to the rose. Students can use this model to write THE SHARK IN MY OCEAN or THE CLAM AT MY SEASHORE or any other creature in its natural habitat. Special aspects of plant and/or animal life can be reported using the patterns found in SLOW CREATURES by Ernest Prescott (Watts 1976), THE TRUTH ABOUT THE MOON by Clayton Bess (Houghton Mifflin 1983), WHAT'S THAT NOISE by Michele Lemieux (Morrow 1985) or A BAG FULL OF PUPS by Dick Gackenbach (Clarion 1981).

REPORTING ABOUT PEOPLE AND PLACES

MARTIN'S HATS by Joan Blos (Morrow 1984) shows young Martin trying out a different hat on each page. Here is a great model for a guessing book. On one page the student could show the shoe, or workplace, or vehicle of a particular worker and let the reader guess the owner. The next page could show the owner and tell a little about that particular occupation.

In MRS. HUGGINS AND HER HEN HANNAH (Dutton 1985) author Lydia Dabcovich shows many of the tasks that must be done on a farm. Using this same idea the student can create a character and the character's pet and show the tasks that would be performed in a lighthouse, or a weather station, a firehouse or on a ranch.

BIOGRAPHY/HISTORY

A variety of product models exist to add excitement to research in both history and biography. One of the best is the narrative poem. After researching the life of a famous person or the facts of an historical event, writing a narrative poem about the person or event can be an exciting challenge. Two excellent examples for students to see as models are THE MICROSCOPE by Maxine Kumin (Harper & Row, 1984) which tells of the life of Anton Leeuwenhock, and PAUL REVERE'S RIDE by Henry Wadsworth Longfellow (Illustrated by Nancy Winslow Parker, Greenwillow, 1985). Another excellent model for reporting history is Judith Viorst's IF I WERE IN CHARGE OF THE WORLD (Atheneum, 1983). In this poem the author muses about how things would be added, or cancelled if she were in charge of the world. The same pattern can be used for reporting places or events in history. IF I WERE IN CHARGE OF A WAGON TRAIN ON THE OREGON TRAIL or IF I WERE IN CHARGE OF THE MAYFLOWER are examples of topics.

Many models of "How To" books abound. These can be analyzed to get ideas for the format of the student's own "how to" book: HOW TO DIG A HOLE TO THE OTHER SIDE OF THE WORLD by Faith McNulty (Harper & Row 1979), HOW A HOUSE HAPPENS by Jan Adkins (Walker 1972) STEVE CANEY'S INVENTION BOOK (Workman 1985) LIGHTS, CAMERA, ACTION by Gail Gibbons (Crowell 1985).

REPORTING IN PICTURES

For students who have problems with the written report, the photo essay can be an excellent means of reporting information. Photographs with a camera or illustrated picture essays can be done. Good examples of product models are: ANIMALS OF COURSE: MOUTHS, NOSES, FEET and EYES by Jill Bailey (Grossett 1985), GOING WEST by Martin Waddell (Harper & Row 1984) and WATCHING FOXES by Jim Arnosky (Lothrop 1985).

RECORD BOOKS

Most students are familiar with the GUINNESS BOOK OF WORLD RECORDS and are eager to try compiling their own record books. A record book can be made on any topic from animals to space travel. Good examples of record books for students to study are HOW HIGH IS UP by Bernice Kohn, a book of interesting questions and answers; HOW LONG? TO GO, TO GROW, TO KNOW by Ross and Patricia Olney (Morrow 1984) and IN ONE DAY by Tom Parker which tells many things which happen in one day in the United States. Using these patterns students could do a record book about their class. Each class member has been somewhere, done something, has a hobby, knows something, that no one else can claim. Ambitious classes might do an IN ONE DAY book about the school, keeping records of all kinds for two or three weeks on as many aspects of the school as possible. For example: How many pencils are sharpened in our school in one day? How many times does the phone ring? How many students are late?

A quick survey of library/media collections will reveal many more product models that will serve as patterns for changing students' research products. In combining the research process with the opportunity to produce something new students cannot help but gain both knowledge of the skills and information needed and of themselves as creative individuals. THE RESEARCH PROJECT BOOK will start students on the road to productive research and serve as a guide for these creative and productive projects.

LOOKING AT TOPIC IDEAS

Before you determine one specific topic for research it is often useful to examine several topics in terms of past, present and future.

Example: AN APPLE

IT WAS _____ once a seed in the ground _____

IT IS _____ a delicious edible fruit _____

IT COULD BE applesauce, apple pie _____

Play with several topic ideas in this way by completing the boxes below. Select the one which most appeals to you. You now have a framework for your project – a beginning, a middle and an end.

TOPIC	IT WAS...	IT IS ...	IT COULD BE...

PROJECTS

TO BUILD A WORKING

VOCABULARY

PUNIDDLES

pun·id·dle   (pŭn·ĭd′·l)

n. 1. A pair of photographs that suggest a literal or obvious solution in a punny way. 2. *pl.* A game using the pair of photographs to deduce the punny solution. [Source: pun, riddle]

The creators of the book PUNIDDLES have combined two photographs to illustrate a simple word.

You can do the same either by taking your own photographs or by finding pictures in old magazines to cut out and combine in new ways.

Bruce and Brett McMillan
Photography by Bruce McMillan

Houghton Mifflin Company   Boston   1982

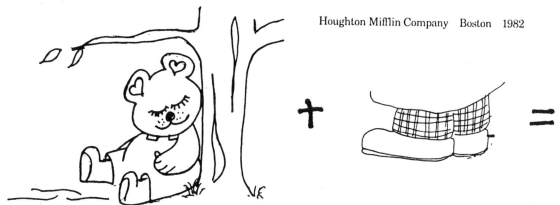

List as many compound words as you can. How many can you illustrate with pairs of photographs? Make your own book of puniddles!

_____ _____   _____ _____

_____ _____   _____ _____

_____ _____   _____ _____

_____ _____   _____ _____

_____ _____   _____ _____

_____ _____   _____ _____

_____ _____   _____ _____

A Bag Full of Pups

By Dick Gackenbach

Clarion Books   1981

1. Name as many of one kind of animal as you can. (birds, fish, cats)

2. Group those you named by the way in which they are useful to man.

RESEARCHING AND REPORTING ON ITEMS WITHIN ONE CATEGORY.

In this book, Mr. Mullens has a bag full of pups to give away. Those who take the pups do so because each dog provides a specific service for its new owner. These owners are:

A DAIRY FARMER

A MAGICIAN

A BLIND PERSON

A LONELY LADY

A FIREMAN

A POLICEMAN

A GROCER

A DOG TRAINER

A HUNTER

3. THINK ABOUT A STORY IN WHICH YOU BRING THE BIRD, FISH OR ANIMAL TOGETHER WITH A PERSON WHO NEEDS IT.

POSSIBLE TITLES

A STABLE FULL OF HORSES

AN OCEAN (OR LAKE OR RIVER) FULL OF FISH

A BACKYARD FULL OF INSECTS

A ZOO FULL OF SNAKES

A FOREST FULL OF BIRDS

THE ROSE IN MY GARDEN IS A wonderful introduction to the flowering world! Each new flower appears on a new page and is added to those which appeared earlier. At the end of the book we see the entire garden.

Select an environmental setting. This might be an ocean, a desert, a mountain, a seashore, a lake, a forest or woodland or any other setting you wish to research.

Research the setting you have chosen. Make lists of the many living and non living things found in that setting. Note the ORDER found in the setting. Which things are usually found together?

Decide on the one living or non living thing you will choose to begin your cumulative tale. What happens to that thing? How can adding other elements of the environment help the first thing you mention in some way? What surprise ending will you use for your story?

THE ROSE IN MY GARDEN
ARNOLD LOBEL
Pictures by ANITA LOBEL

'This is the rose in my garden.
This is the bee
that sleeps on the rose in my garden."

And so begins the horticultural panoply—a cumulative verse involving hollyhocks, marigolds, zinnias, daisies, bluebells, lilies, peonies, pansies, tulips, and sunflowers—and a surprise.

POSSIBLE TOPICS TO RESEARCH

The Jellyfish in My Ocean

The Clam At My Seashore

The Rattlesnake in My Desert

The Fir Tree on My Mountain

The Seed in the Farmer's Field

The Catfish in My Lake

The Trout in My River

The Woodchuck in My Woodland

The Desk in My Classroom

The Worm in My Backyard

THE ROSE IN MY GARDEN is published by Greenwillow Books, 1984.

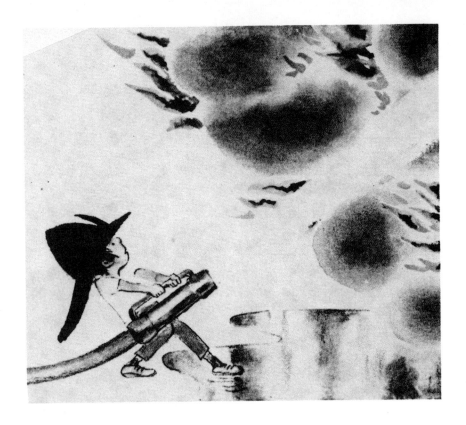

FINDING A FOCUS

IN

RESEARCHING AND

REPORTING   ON

CAREERS

AND/OR

OCCUPATIONS

In this model the author
and illustrator show the
many kinds of hats used
in a variety of jobs.

CHOOSE A GROUP OF
OCCUPATIONS

FIND A FOCUS!

WHAT WILL YOU SHOW?

　　TOOLS

　　CLOTHING

　　WORKPLACES

MARTIN'S HATS

JOAN W. BLOS
Illustrated by MARC SIMONT

From a real explorer's hat that takes him through dark caves . . . to the
striped engineer's cap he wears to drive a train . . . and the hard hat
that's handy when he's welding a girder, Martin dashes, hat by hat,
through a grand round of adventures.

Morrow Junior Books 1984

Your book might be a guessing book. Show particular tools used in various
trades or professions and ask your reader to match the tool with the trades
or professions in which it is most used. Give an explanation as to just how
the tool is used. OR match jobs with the place where they are performed.

On one page show the tool, clothing or workplace and list several workers.
Ask your reader which worker would use the tool, wear the clothing or
be found in the workplace.

On the page following give the correct answer and explain how the worker
uses the tool; why a particular item of clothing is important; or why the
worker needs the workplace shown to do his or her job.

A Child's Guide To Conflict Resolution
HOW TO TURN WAR INTO Peace
by Louise Armstrong
illustrated by Bill Basso

Harcourt, Brace, Jovanovich 1979

UNDERSTANDING LAW VOCABULARY

By telling of a disagreement between two children building sandcastles on a beach, Louise Armstrong illustrates the vocabulary of conflict.

The story begins:
This is Susie. If she's building her sandcastle right next to yours, you're in a POTENTIAL TROUBLE SPOT. Susie's digging might clog your moat creating an INCIDENT. If you yell, "move!"-you have a DISPUTE.
Susie is your ADVERSARY.

Study the way in which this author cleverly introduces the vocabulary of conflict. Below are words dealing with rules and laws.

CREATE AN ILLUSTRATED STORY
WHICH INTRODUCES THIS VOCABULARY
OF LAW AND RULES

accused	fairness	minors
authority	freedom	
		petition
bail	impartiality	power
		press
citizens	judge	privacy
correction of wrongs	juris prudence	property
court	jury	protection
	justice	
due process		regulations
	laws	responsibility
equality	lawyer	rights
equal protection	legal system	rules
equity		

13

Tyrannosaurus Wrecks

A Book of Dinosaur Riddles
by Noelle Sterne Pictures by Victoria Chess

FROM

RESEARCH

TO

RIDDLES!

USING

RIDDLE

MAKING

TO

BUILD

WORD

POWER!

Thomas Y. Crowell Publishers   © 1979

THE MORE YOU KNOW ABOUT A TOPIC, THE MORE RIDDLES YOU CAN MAKE.

HERE IS THE SECRET FOR WRITING RIDDLES:

1) CHOOSE A TOPIC AND MAKE A LONG LIST OF AS MANY WORDS AS YOU CAN THAT ARE ASSOCIATED WITH THAT TOPIC.

   (Example: TOPIC: PIGS Words: ham, pen, pork. slop, Porky,. swine swill, mud, porcine, sow, shoat, piglet)

2) CHOOSE ONE OR TWO SHORT WORDS FROM YOUR LIST AND REMOVE THE BEGINNING LETTER OR BEGINNING BLEND.

   (Example: HAM- remove the H and you have AM
   SLOP-remove the SL and you have OP

3) LIST AS MANY WORDS AS YOU CAN WHICH BEGIN WITH THE LETTERS AM. LIST WORDS THAT BEGIN WITH THE LETTERS OP. EXAMINE YOUR LISTS.

4) WRITE YOUR RIDDLES : PUT BACK THE MISSING LETTER(S) FOR THE ANSWER.

   Example: WHAT TAKES A PIG TO THE HOSPITAL ? a HAMBULANCE

   WHAT DO YOU CALL A PIG THAT WORKS FOR THE PHONE COMPANY?   a SLOPERATOR.

TRY WRITING RIDDLES BASED ON A TOPIC YOU HAVE RESEARCHED.

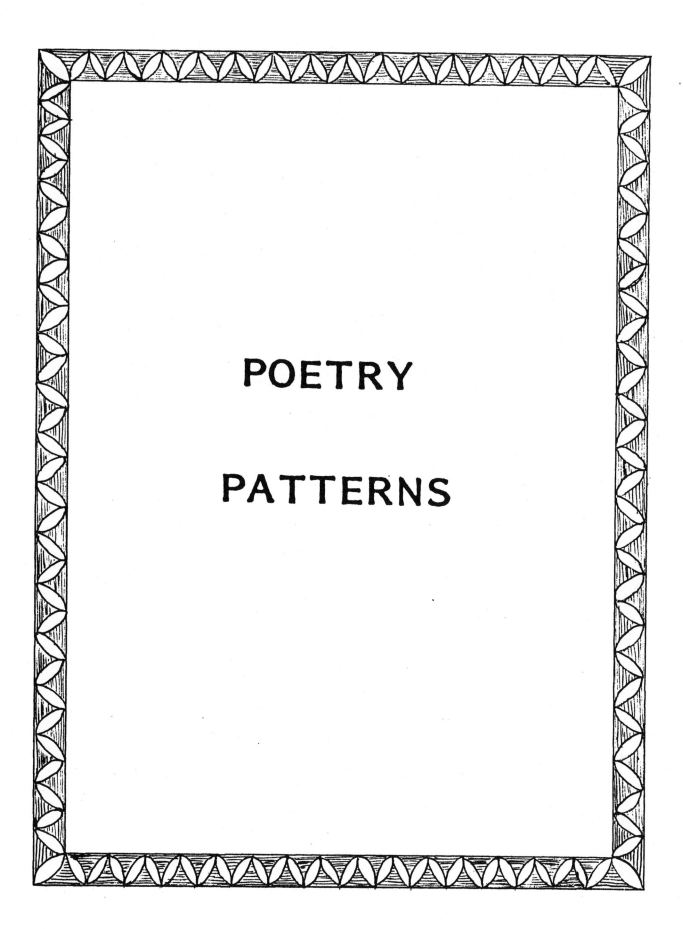

POETRY

PATTERNS

Plants That Never Ever Bloom
Written and illustrated by Ruth Heller
Grosset and Dunlap, 1984

Here is a delightful model to use in reporting research on a non-fiction topic! Author-artist, Ruth Heller tells of non-flowering plants in both pictures and verse.

"In the Pacific and Atlantic
Seaweed grows to be gigantic.
This mass has broken free
And floats in the Sargasso Sea,
Where grumpy looking fish reside,
And other creatures like to hide."

What topic might you research to tell about in verse?

What important facts can you include?

How will you illustrate your book?

Study this model carefully for ideas!

<u>Come Along</u>
By Rebecca Caudill
Illustrated by Ellen Haskin
Holt, Rinehart and Winston, 1969

The author takes the reader through the seasons, the mountain, and the meadow. She uses Haiku verse to give the reader vivid descriptions.

"Two doves in a wood
Coo softly to each other
Celebrating spring."

Haiku verse consists of seventeen syllables. Lines one and three each contain five syllables and line two contains seven syllables.

Take A Trip

Take your reader on a trip using the model of Haiku verse above.

Possible trips

up a mountain   into the desert
out to sea   into the ocean depths
across the tundra   up into the sky

What to do:

1. Decide what kind of trip you want your reader to take through your writing.

2. Read about the area you wish to use.

3. List several words describing the area.

4. Organize your words into Haiku verse using this model.

5. Write a story using Haiku verse and illustrate as many scenes as possible.

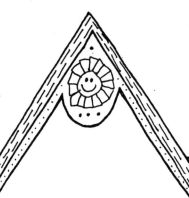

A House Is a House for Me

MARY ANN HOBERMAN
Illustrated by BETTY FRASER
Viking 1978

POETRY PATTERNS

In her delightful book-length poem, Mary Ann Hoberman explores houses used by many of the Earth's creatures.

"A kennel is a house
  for a dog,
A dog is a house
  for a flea.
But when the dog
  strays,
The flea sometimes stays,
And then it may move in
  on me!"

Use this poetry model to research and report on what the Earth's creatures eat. Choose six to eight creatures for your poem.

EXAMPLE

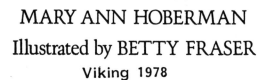

_____ is a food for a cat.

_____ is food for a bee.

_____ is food for a worm

but _____ is food for me.

A _____ likes to eat _____.

A _____ eats up some _____.

A _____ prefers _____ and _____

But I like to eat _____ _____.

Paul Revere's Ride

HENRY WADSWORTH
LONGFELLOW
Pictures by
NANCY WINSLOW PARKER

Since it was written in 1863, generations of children have read, recited, and loved Longfellow's classic poem. Here is the full text of this dramatization of an important incident in America's history, profusely and lovingly illustrated for young readers. With each turn of the page the excitement and adventure increase, and the heroic cadences of the poem are perfect for reading aloud again and again.

Greenwillow Books, 1985

THE NARRATIVE POEM
AN
EXCITING WAY TO REPORT ON EVENTS
FROM HISTORY!

Paul Revere's Ride

by

Henry Wadsworth Longfellow

Listen, my children, and you shall hear
Of the midnight ride of Paul Revere,
On the eighteenth of April, in Seventy-five
Hardly a man is now alive
Who remembers that famous day and year.

He said to his friend, "If the British march
By land or sea from the town tonight,
Hang a lantern aloft in the belfry arch
Of the North Church tower as a signal light—

Longfellow (with the help in this book of Nancy Winslow Parker's illustrations) tells of this famous ride with all of its events in the form of a narrative poem.

READ THE ENTIRE POEM.

NOTE HOW EACH EVENT IS PRESENTED.

RESEARCH AN IMPORTANT EVENT FROM HISTORY.

LIST FACTS IN THE ORDER IN WHICH THEY SHOULD APPEAR.

Use PAUL REVERE'S RIDE as a model, write your narrative poem. (Often, schools discard older history textbooks. If these are available you can illustrate your poem with photographs or drawings from these texts.)

REPORTING ON PLACES

The place where one lives as either a child or an adult can be important to that person's life. The sights and sounds at Buckingham Palace would be very different from the sights and sounds at Thomas Jefferson's Monticello.

Research the home of a famous person or the location of an event from history. Write about it using the pattern below.

This is the place
where _____ (lives) (works)
(fights) (other)
This is where

_____
_____.

This is where

_____
_____.

And you can hear _____
_____.

And you can see _____
_____.

And you can feel _____
_____.

And _____ cares.

REPORTING

RESEARCH

WITH

POETRY!

In the introductory
poem in this fun
collection Judith
Viorst plays with the
idea of what she
would do if she were
in charge of the
world. In the poem
the poet:
  Cancels four things
  Adds three things
  Tells five things
  "you wouldn't have"
  And ends with
  three things that
  might happen.

ALADDIN

Atheneum A145 $3.95

IF I WERE IN CHARGE OF THE WORLD

and other worries

poems for children and their parents by
JUDITH VIORST
ILLUSTRATED BY LYNNE CHERRY

Atheneum, 1983

Using this poem as a reporting model, research one thing you would like to
be in charge of: (The Mayflower: The space shuttle? Your state?)

IF I WERE IN CHARGE OF _____

I'd cancel	There'd be	You wouldn't have
_____	_____	_____
_____	_____	_____
_____	_____	_____
_____	_____	_____

Add a final verse telling what else <u>might</u> happen!

REPORTING
DISCOVERIES IN VERSE!

With lighthearted humor, author
and artist re-create for young readers
Leeuwenhoek's bustling 17th-
century Dutch world as well as the
small, fascinating, never-before-
seen world his own microscopes
revealed.

Anton Leeuwenhoek
was Dutch.
He sold pincushions,
cloth, and such.
The waiting townsfolk
fumed and fussed,
as Anton's dry goods
gathered dust.
He worked,
instead of tending store,
at grinding special lenses for
a microscope.

THE MICROSCOPE
by Maxine Kumin Pictures by Arnold Lobel

Harper & Row , Publishers
Jacket art © 1984 by Arnold Lobel

How many discoveries can you name in any category below?

AGRICULTURE	MEDICINE	CATEGORY
ASTRONOMY	PSYCHOLOGY	_____
ANTHROPOLOGY	TECHNOLOGY	DISCOVERIES
BIOLOGY	TRANSPORTATION	_____
EXPLORATION	COMMUNICATION	_____
		_____
		_____

Select one discovery. Who made the discovery? Research that person's life
and work. Recreate the discovery in verse form for others to enjoy.

COMBINING BIOGRAPHY AND INCIDENTS FROM HISTORY

Often, incidents in the lives of famous people give clues to their personalities and to their later accomplishments.

Below is an acrostic poem which describes an incident in the life of Winston Churchill. From reading about this incident, an assumption might be made that the abilities of being able to size up a situation and the courage to risk success played an important part in Churchill's later accomplishments as Prime Minister of Great Britain during World War II.

Use this model to report an incident in the life of another famous person.

W ar correspondent

I n South Africa, 1899

N ortorious Boer enemy

S eizes armored

T rain

O f those aboard, he is captured.

N o hope of escape.

C hecks out prison camp.

H igh walls, floodlights, sentries.

U p, over the wall, in an unguarded moment

R acing heart, he scales the heights.

C amp left behind.

H opping railroad cars

I n dead of night finds British help.

L auded as a hero.

L eader of the future.

THE STORY POEM

Here is an acrostic poem relating an incident in the childhood of George Gershwin. He grew up in a non-musical family on New York's east side. To survive there he had to be a fighter. He disliked school in general and music class in particular. Yet, George Gershwin, who became one of the world's most beloved composers, credited his entrance into the world of music with an incident that happened to him at the age of ten. The poem below relates this event.

Growing up, picking fights,

Ear for music, NONE!

Only sissies play pianos

Rubenstein was one.

Going past the arcade, Melody in F

Entered George's hearing, stopped by Treble Cleff!

Going past school window, music from within

Enchanted by a melody, played on violin.

Rooted to the spot, hearing tiny Maxie play

Sad and haunting melody, George again was forced to stay.

He made friends with the fiddler, and at the age of ten

World's of music opened, he studied hard and then

Intensely innovative music flowed forth from his heart

NOW lauded by the critics, a composer set apart.

Read about Gershwin's life. The road to fame was not easy! Using the acrostic form above, relate another incident that may have been a turning point in his life.

The <u>Wounded</u> <u>Wolf</u> by Jean Craighead George, Harper and Row, 1978.

Jean George is a careful observer of nature. You don't have to go to far off places to be a careful observer as well.

1. Be a patient observer. Observe the animal, worm, bird or insect you have chosen very carefully. Take notes on its behavior for one or more weeks.

2. Look for behavior that is repeated. Ask yourself why it is repeated. What happens to the creature before or after the behavior?

3. Write a story in words and pictures telling of a typical day in the creature's life.

4. If possible, begin your story by telling of a problem the creature has. End the story by solving the problem.

Notice how Jean George begins her book with a problem.

> "A wounded wolf climbs Toklat Ridge,
> a massive spine of rock and ice.
> As he limps, dawn strikes the ridge
> and lights it up with sparks and stars."

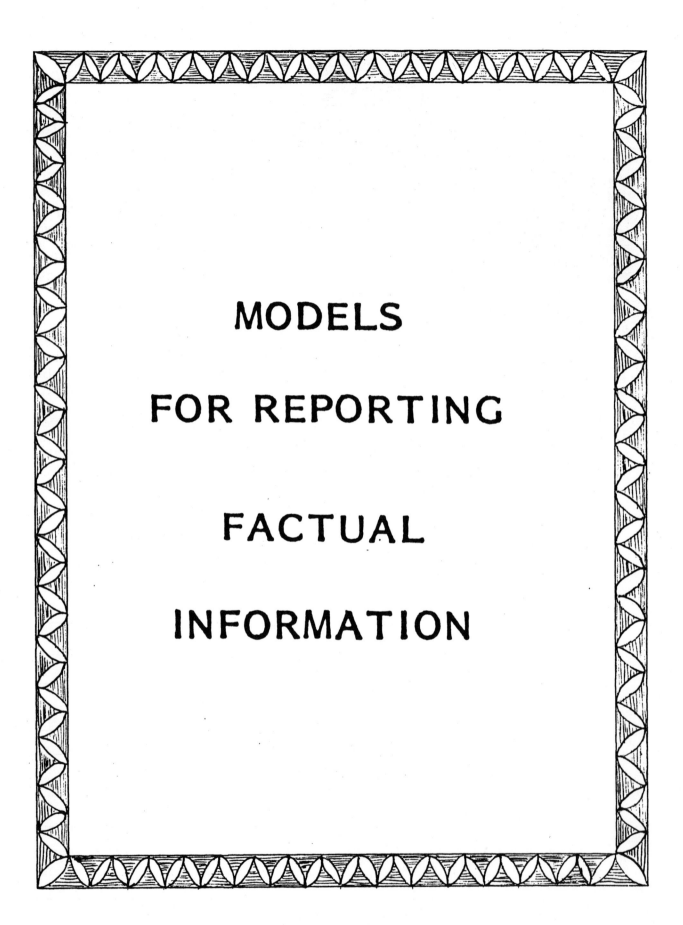

MODELS

FOR REPORTING

FACTUAL

INFORMATION

RESEARCH ON ONE TOPIC

or

How To Tell Others All About Your Favorite Subject

An excellent model to examine if you want to give others information on your favorite subject is <u>Maps and Globes</u> by Jack Knowlton. (Thomas Y. Crowell, 1985)

In this book you learn twenty one different things about maps and globes. Each topic appears on a new, illustrated page. Some of the topics are: "Maps put our round earth on flat paper" and "Maps have a language you can learn."

List your favorite topic _____

What ten interesting questions will you answer for your reader?

1. _____
2. _____
3. _____
4. _____
5. _____
6. _____
7. _____
8. _____
9. _____
10. _____

Use one page to answer each question in words and pictures. Design a title page and staple your book together for others to enjoy.

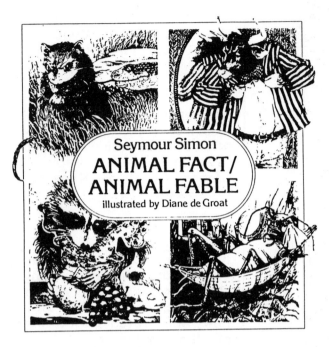

Seymour Simon
ANIMAL FACT/
ANIMAL FABLE
illustrated by Diane de Groat

Crown Publishers 1979

FACT OR FABLE?

Here is a colorful and informative picture book to test your knowledge about animals.

Each page poses a question which is answered on the next page.

In this book you will discover whether these and other statements are fact or fable.

BATS ARE BLIND.

SOME BEES STING ONLY ONCE.

AN OWL IS A WISE BIRD.

THE ARCHER FISH SHOOTS DOWN ITS FOOD.

A TURTLE CAN WALK OUT OF ITS SHELL.

SOME FISH CAN CLIMB TREES.

A WOLF LIVES ALONE.

CAMELS STORE WATER IN THEIR HUMPS.

What to do:

1. Begin researching "truths" that parents often say.

   Example: If you eat your bread crusts you can whistle.
   Spinach will make you strong.

2. Collect as many sayings as you can from friends.

3. Discover whether the saying is fact or fable.

4. Using Seymour Simon's Animal Fact/Animal Fable as your guide, write and illustrate your book.
   On one page give the saying. On the next page tell whether it is fact or fable and give an explanation.

5. Share your book with others.

REPORTING ON ONE ASPECT OF AN ANIMAL

Slow Creatures
By Ernest Prescott
Franklin Watts, 1976

All animals must eat to stay alive. They must also protect themselves from other animals. To do these things most creatures have something special about them. Elephants are big. Lions are strong. Antelopes are fast.

But what about creatures who are slow? Can being slow have its good points? A snail is slow, but it has a hard shell to protect itself. A chameleon is a slow moving lizard, but it can change colors to hide from its enemies. The Gila monster is slow but uses poison to attack his enemies. Some animals may be slow but have effective ways to protect themselves.

Can you think of a group of animals who have something in common? Create an informative booklet of these creatures.

Possible Topics

Fast Creatures
Creatures who live in the ocean
Creatures who live in the jungle
Creatures who live in the desert
Creatures who live in the lake
Creatures which change colors

What to do:

1. Choose ten animals from the same category.

2. Write the interesting facts about the animals.

3. Use illustrations or cut out pictures of these animals from magazines to use in your booklet.

A SENSE AND
NONSENSE MODEL

Seymour Simon has used the subject of computers for an interesting and most informative true/false book.

The book contains twenty-four statements about computers and challenges the reader to decide whether each statement is sense or nonsense.

Some of the provocative statements are:

Computers can take over the world.
Computers never forget.
Computer's can't see, hear or talk.
Computers can smell flowers.

Illustrated by Steven Lindblom

J.B. Lippincott 1984

1. Select a subject of interest to you.

2. Read about the subject.

3. Make notes of unusual or interesting information.

4. Decide how many sense and nonsense statements will be in your book. Be sure to include both.

5. Use one page to write and illustrate a statement.

6. Use the next page to explain whether the statement is sense or nonsense.

BODY SENSE, BODY NONSENSE

DOES AN APPLE A DAY KEEP THE DOCTOR AWAY?

ARE CARROTS GOOD FOR YOUR EYESIGHT?

CAN HOLDING YOUR BREATH CURE HICCUPS?

by Seymour Simon

illustrated by Dennis Kendrick

J.B. Lippincott   New York

J. B. Lippincott, 1981

PICK A TOPIC
     WRITE YOUR OWN SENSE
OR NONSENSE BOOK.

Write your own true/false book using as your model Seymour Simon's, Body Sense, Body Nonsense.

In this book the author asks the reader whether a statement is sense or nonsense. On the next page the answer and an explanation are given.

Examples:
     Sense or Nonsense?

An apple a day keeps the doctor away.

Redheads have bad tempers.

Drafts cause colds.

Fish is brain food.

Science

Bird Sense, Bird Nonsense
Mammal Sense, Mammal Nonsense
Planet Sense, Planet Nonsense
Chemistry Sense, Chemistry Nonsense
Dinosaur Sense, Dinosaur Nonsense
Atomic Sense, Atomic Nonsense
Sound Sense, Sound Nonsense

History/Geography

Desert Sense, Desert Nonsense
U.S. Sense, U.S. Nonsense
Canadian Sense, Canadian Nonsense
Gold Rush Sense, Gold Rush Nonsense
WW II Sense, WW II Nonsense
People Sense, People Nonsense

A FIVE SENSES REPORT

In her book, <u>Science</u> <u>Experiences</u> <u>THE</u> <u>HUMAN</u> <u>SENSES</u>, (Franklin Watts, 1968) Jeanne Bendick tells how we learn by using our five senses.

When we find ourselves in a new place, we learn about that place by SEEING SIGHTS, HEARING SOUNDS, SMELLING ODORS, TASTING FOOD and TOUCHING OBJECTS.

In your report you can help others to experience new places by describing sights, sounds, tastes, smells and feelings.

A Circus

Color:	A circus is many bright colors.
Looks like:	It looks like a patchwork quilt.
Sounds like:	It sounds like six record players going all at once.
Smells like:	It smells like sawdust.
Tastes like:	It tastes like cotton candy.
It makes me feel like:	It makes me feel like laughing.

Choose

A zoo

A firehouse

A hospital

A bakery

A post office

A grocery store

Write your report.

_____
Title

Color: _____

Looks like: _____

Sounds like: _____

Smells like: _____

Tastes like: _____

It makes me feel like: _____

_____

Read about the place you choose.

The Lady and the Spider

by Faith McNulty

illustrated by Bob Marstall

Harper & Row, Publishers
1986

A spider has made her home among the green hills and valleys of a lettuce leaf. It is a perfect den, just the right size, with a dewdrop pool nearby that will catch moths on moonlit nights. What the spider cannot know is that her home is in a lady's garden.

Each day the lady comes to pick lettuce for her lunch. Each day she comes a little closer to the spider's cozy nook without ever guessing that her giant footsteps shake the spider's little home.

Then one day the lady picks the very head of lettuce in which the spider lives. When at last she notices the spider frantically trying to escape, the lady stops just short of carelessly destroying the tiny creature and begins to marvel at its fragile existence— and to think about the miracle of things large and small.

Harper & Row, Publishers

What encounters have YOU had that you want to share with others? Have you met a person you would like to tell about? Did you observe something very interesting that you want to relate? In describing YOUR encounter consider?

1. When and where did the encounter take place?
2. How old were you at the time?
3. What did you see, hear, feel?
4. How did the encounter affect you?
5. What could others learn from reading about this encounter?

If you prefer to report your information in a different format, consider making a tape with background music to play for your class or audience. If you have slides of a trip you have taken you may want to write a script which blends fact and fiction to accompany the slides.

Use this model to take your readers on a trip through a particular environment and motivate readers to WANT to take the trip by allowing them to find something unusual at the end of the journey!

POSSIBLE TRIPS

JOURNEY TO THE MOON

JOURNEY TO THE OCEAN FLOOR

JOURNEY TO MR. MACGREGOR'S GARDEN

JOURNEY THROUGH A DESERT

JOURNEY THROUGH A COAL MINE

JOURNEY THROUGH A PYRAMID

JOURNEY TO EPCOT OR DISNEY WORLD

JOURNEY THROUGH A DEPARTMENT STORE

JOURNEY THROUGH A POLICE STATION

JOURNEY ON THE OREGON TRAIL

JOURNEY THROUGH ANOTHER STATE

JOURNEY THROUGH ANOTHER COUNTRY

What's That Noise?

MICHÈLE LEMIEUX

Waking from a deep sleep, Brown Bear wonders, What's that noise? It's not the *squeak-squeak* that little mice make or the *peep-peep* of baby birds in their nests. It's not the noise the frogs by the stream make or the *chock-chock* of the woodsman's ax. What is that noise? Through the shady green of a springtime forest, the sunlit fields of summer, and the golden harvest of fall, the curious bear searches and finds a wonderful surprise. Young children everywhere will share the bear's delight in his own special moment of self-discovery.

Morrow Junior Books 1985

WHAT TO DO:

1. Read, read, read about your topic!
2. List all of the important words or ideas you want to present to your reader.
3. Place your words or ideas in the order in which you want to present them.
4. Decide on a main character for your story.
5. Decide what that character will be seeking.
6. Decide where the thing being sought will be found.
7. Write your story taking your character through each part of the trip.
8. Make the ending (when the object is found) a surprise.
9. Illustrate your story if possible.

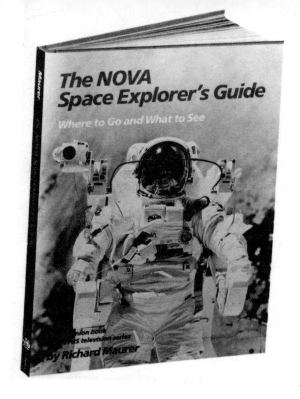

A GUIDE BOOK
TO AN UNUSUAL PLACE

In THE NOVA SPACE EXPLORER'S GUIDE, author Richard Maurer unfolds NOVA'S journey into space with more than 200 photographs and illustrations.

After an introduction to rockets past and present, the reader climbs aboard a space ship for a fabulous visit to lunar mountains, Mercury's volcanos, the outer planets of Jupiter and Pluto, and continues on into the galaxy to tour the stars.

Throughout this breath-taking trip, details of the space flight are given, including equipment needed and living arrangements.

Have you recently taken a trip?

Do you plan to take a trip soon?

Is your family involved in an unusual business that others might want to know about?

Write and illustrate a guidebook for YOUR reader. Remember, details are very important to give your reader a clear view of the place you are describing.

Cover illustration from
THE NOVA SPACE
EXPLORER'S GUIDE
by Richard Maurer
Crown 1984

WRITE AND ILLUSTRATE A GUIDEBOOK

Consider:
The Zoo Explorer's Guide
The Fire House Explorer's Guide
The Library Explorer's Guide

An Explorer's Guide to Our Town
An Explorer's Guide to the Local
    Shopping Center

Choose one of the topics above or select your own topic.

BE SURE TO TELL:

1. Where the reader is going, what special clothing or equipment he or she will need, and how long the trip will be.
2. What sights, sounds, smells are present at the site.
3. If people are present at the site, tell their jobs.
4. Use plenty of illustrations. These can be photographs, pictures cut from old magazines or your own illustrations. Think of a good caption for each illustration.

A DAY IN THE LIFE OF _____

A Day In The Life of a Television News Reporter
By William Jaspersohn
Little, Brown and Company, 1981

This is a story about Dan Rea who loves the reporting life. His day starts with a walk to the mail room and a stop by the newsroom. The newsroom is always busy with typewriters clicking. A stop to see the news director and the producer are next. There are several hours of work before the news can be put on the air for viewing by the general public.

News Reporters

News reporters have many tasks to complete before they are ready to face the public. There are many people involved in the preparation of the day's news. There are many machines and technical problems involved in the production of a news show.

Directions

1. Choose a famous person in history.
   Examples: President Kennedy
              Prince Charles
              Christopher Columbus

2. List all the support people behind your famous person who helped make his/her accomplishments a success.

3. List any machines or technical advances that made his/her jobs easier.

4. Write a story with illustrations and use the title: A Day In the Life of _____. (Fill in the name of the famous person you have chosen). Use the same model as the book mentioned on this page.

A LETTER-WRITING PROJECT

The authors of <u>Free Stuff for Kids</u> have gathered information from many organizations and businesses about free materials they give away.

On each page of this book you are told:

Where to write.

What to ask for.

Postage and/or handling charges.

Meadowbrook Press
Wayzata, MN 55391

THE SECOND RAINBOW BOOK

By Pat Blakely, Barbara Haislet, & Judith Hentges

Compile A State or Community "Free Stuff" Book

1) Determine the kinds of materials you want to include. (Print, nonprint, all free, some with small charges, specific subject areas, materials for older or younger children).

2) Analyze the major subject areas you want to include. What organizations or businesses deal with these subjects? Both the yellow pages and the lists of organizations in the almanac can help here.

3) Compose a letter asking about the availability of free materials and procedure (s) for obtaining the materials. Ask for samples of the materials to examine.

4) Compile your data in booklet form. Be sure to include all necessary information your reader will need to have to obtain the material.

CAUSES

AND

A soft drink has about **9** teaspoons of sugar
A candy bar has about **7** teaspoons of sugar
A piece of chocolate cake has about **7** teaspoons of sugar
A milkshake has about **7** teaspoons of sugar
A plain doughnut has about **4** teaspoons of sugar
A cup of sugared cereal has about **4** teaspoons of sugar
A brownie has about **3** teaspoons of sugar

Greenwillow Books 1984

EFFECTS

Most people know that junk food is not healthful. However, junk food is eaten more by people than almost any other kind of food.

List reasons why (causes) people eat junk food.

_____

_____

_____

_____

_____

_____

What effects will be noticed from eating too much junk food?

_____

_____

_____

JUNK FOOD— WHAT IT IS, WHAT IT DOES

JUDITH S. SEIXAS
Pictures by TOM HUFFMAN

The author of *Alcohol—What It Is, What It Does* now provides another informative, easy to read and understand manual on a vitally important subject. Tailored for the audience that needs it most, here are the facts they should know on what junk food is and why it is bad for them.

Select a topic for research and report on the topic by giving as many causes and effects of of the topic as you can.

POSSIBLE TOPIC

TELEVISION: WHAT IT IS WHAT IT DOES

Research what caused television to become such an important part of our lives.

Research the effects (what it does) of television on different parts of the population.

OTHER POSSIBLE TOPICS

INFLATION: WHAT IT IS (causes) WHAT IT DOES (effects)

DRUGS: WHAT THEY ARE, WHAT THEY DO

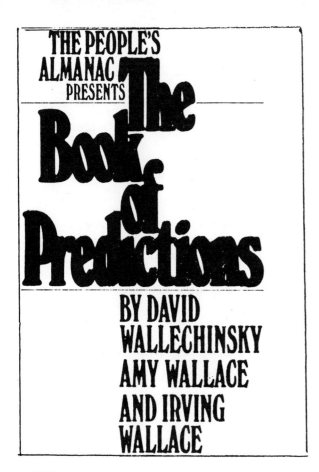

THE PEOPLE'S ALMANAC PRESENTS The Book of Predictions

BY DAVID WALLECHINSKY AMY WALLACE AND IRVING WALLACE

William Morrow Publishers, 1980

IS IT POSSIBLE TO PREDICT THE FUTURE?

These people would say yes!

BUSINESS ANALYST

DEMOGRAPHER

PHYSICIAN

WALL STREET ANALYST

Study the predictions below. Some were made by experts in their fields. Others were made by psychics. Can you tell which is which?

Select one prediction for research. From your research gather evidence to SUPPORT OR DENY THE VALIDITY OF THE PREDICTION.

IF POSSIBLE, RESEARCH ONE SOCIAL ASPECT OF YOUR COMMUNITY. PREDICT FUTURE TRENDS. DEMONSTRATE WITH A GRAPH.

Example: Future building trends
Size of school population
Most popular means of transportation
New businesses

Predictions

1988 The track record for the mile is 3 min. 32 sec.

1989 A computer makes an original scientific discovery and its program is nominated for a Nobel Prize.

1990 Areas of Texas and California split off to form new states. Wrist telephones are popular. Artificial eyesight is invented for blind people.

1993 After a U.S. stock market crash and major depression, the United States ceases to be a great power.

2000 All Persian Gulf countries run out of oil.

2002 If caught in the early stages, every kind of cancer is now curable.

2010 International terrorists, employing nuclear weapons, destroy a major world capital. This leads to police repression, which in turn leads to a worldwide disarmament conference. As a result, nuclear-weapon systems are scrapped.

2030 A democratic United States of the World is established.

"THE EARTH IS FLAT"—AND OTHER GREAT MISTAKES

ʙʏ LAURENCE PRINGLE

ILLUSTRATED BY STEVE MILLER

William Morrow 1984

GREAT MISTAKES!

In this book Laurence Pringle has collected some of the greatest mistakes made by people throughout history. At the same time he gives basic reasons why people make mistakes. They are:

1. Lack of knowledge

2. Ignoring the facts

4. Taking a risk

The mistakes in this book range from constructing a skyscraper with windows that pop out in a strong wind to the sinking of the Titanic.

Your Book of Great Mistakes

1. Interview family, teachers and friends about the greatest mistake each has made. Try to determine the reason for the mistake and include this in each account.

2. Compile a book about these great mistakes.

3. Illustrate your book if possible.

4. Your book should be one of the most read books in your school!

BIOGRAPHY REPORT

Subject's Name _____

Complete this questionnaire as if you <u>were</u> the subject!

1) If the Pied Piper of Hamlin asked me for money to rid our town of rats, I would:

A) give money gladly
B) work on a committee to raise the money

C) tell him "the more rats the better."
D) say it's not my problem.

2) My favorite books are:

A) fantasy tales
B) adventure tales

C) factual information
D) sports stories

3) I feel it is best in any situation:

A) to plan for it
B) to dream about it

C) to wait and see what happens
D) to take immediate action

4) If I have a problem I prefer:

A) to solve it myself
B) individual counseling

C) group counseling
D) to ignore it

5) I would choose for a pet:

A) a dog
B) a cat

C) a snake
D) an exotic bird

6) I am most efficient in:

A) planning
B) predicting from scientific data

C) descerning the moods of others
D) using intuition as my guide

7) I remember best

A) how to perform a motor skill
B) names

C) faces
D) statistics

8) My best subject in school is/was:
A) speech
B) philosophy

C) math
D) reading

9) I show my feelings:

A) not at all
B) easily

C) in poetry, art or drama
D) only when absolutely necessary

10) My opinion of Sidney Carton in <u>A</u> Tale <u>of</u> <u>Two</u> <u>Cities</u> is that:

A) he was noble
B) he was misguided

C) he was stupid
D) he was too drunk to know what he was doing

TURNING POINTS!

In more than a hundred surprising
revealing and entertaining tales, the
reader relives the creative experiences
of history's most important innovators.
In a trip behind the scenes we learn
about:

THE ACCIDENT THAT CREATED RAYON

THE VISIONS THAT PROPELLED NAT
TURNER TO HIS FATEFUL REBELLION

THE WARM BATH THAT LED TO
ARCHIMEDES' FAMOUS MATHEMATICAL
PRINCIPLE

THE WRITING CONTEST THAT LED TO
MARY SHELLEY'S FRANKENSTEIN

THE SUPERNATURAL INCIDENT THAT
LED HITLER TO POWER

THE CONVERSATION THAT LED HOWARD
MAXIM TO DEVELOP THE MAXIM
MACHINE GUN

Brainstorms &
Thunderbolts

How Creative Genius Works

Carol Orsag Madigan & Ann Elwood

Macmillan Publishing Company

1983

New York

YOUR RESEARCH PRODUCT........................

A BOOK ON TURNING POINTS IN ? ? ?

What to do

1. Select a field of human endeavor of great interest to you.

2. Compile an extensive list of people who have made significant
    contributions to that field.

3. Locate biographical references. Read briefly about those on your list.

4. Select eight to twelve of those who most fascinate you. Research each life
    giving particular attention to TURNING POINTS which led to later significant
    achievement.

5. Tell about each turning point in story form. Illustrate with photos, slides
    or sketches, if possible.

POSSIBLE TOPICS

TURNING POINTS IN THE LIVES OF SCIENTISTS, MILITARY LEADERS,
GOVERNMENTAL LEADERS, INVENTORS, ARTISTS, MUSICIANS, DANCERS,
WRITERS, POETS, SPORTS FIGURES, LABOR LEADERS, JOURNALISTS.

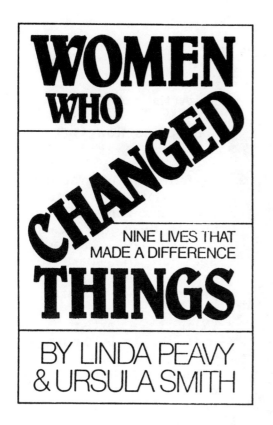

WOMEN WHO CHANGED THINGS

NINE LIVES THAT MADE A DIFFERENCE

BY LINDA PEAVY & URSULA SMITH

SETTING CRITERIA FOR A COLLECTIVE BIOGRAPHY

WOMEN WHO CHANGED THINGS is a collective biography of the lives of nine women. In selecting women for inclusion in this book the authors set the following exacting criteria:

THE WOMEN CHOSEN

1. Must have demonstrably changed the lives of others.

2. Must represent broad ethnic makeup and regional differences.

3. Must have written documentation of lives and achievements.

4. Must represent a wide variety of fields of endeavor.

5. Must have lived between 1880 and 1930

YOUR COLLECTIVE BIOGRAPHY

1) Select an area of focus.

> IDEAS: A) THE GREATEST PROBLEM SOLVED BY ....
>
> B) DECISIONS THAT CHANGED LIVES.
>
> C) TURNING POINTS (IN THE LIVES OF THE GREAT)
>
> D) EARLY FAILURE-LATE SUCCESS

2) Establish written criteria for those who will be included in your book.

3) Research the lives of the people you choose to write about

4) Write the accounts of these lives with particular attention to your area of focus.

5) Share your manuscript with your class.With your school. With your community,perhaps in the form of a weekly newspaper column.

Starter Ideas

Women Who Ruled
Women Who Cared
Women Who Influenced Others

Women in Medicine
Women Freedom Fighters
Women Who Made a Difference

WOMEN WHO CHANGED THINGS is published by Charles Scribner's Sons. 1983

RESEARCHING PERSONALITIES

Illus. from An Artist's Album 1985

<u>An Artist's Album</u>
by M. B. Goffstein
Harper & Row 1985

In four mini-biographies, M.B. Goffstein captures the personality of four artists through revealing images and incidents. See how the spare text captures the spirit of artist, Claude Monet.

"You gave artists new faith in their brushes, paints, and rags.
Loving flowers, you gardened water and land.
Above your round palette, big and balanced as a boat, you might have been a frog taking in the view from a lily pad."

<u>YOUR PROJECT</u>

1. Select four people who have made significant contributions to a particular field.

2. Research their personalities.

3. Note relationship (if any) between personality and accomplishment.

4. Write a poetry portrait of each similar to those given in <u>An Artist's Album</u>.

You can build a better mousetrap.

DISCOVER:

GETTING STARTED IN INVENTING
TOOLS FOR THE INVENTOR'S WORKSHOP
KEEPING NOTEBOOKS (HOW TO)
PLANNING PROCEDURES
NAMING YOUR INVENTION
PATENTS
MARKETING YOUR INVENTION
GREAT INVENTION STORIES

Research the beginnings of one or more inventions detailed in this book.

Predict what would happen if this invention were not now a part of our lives!

Steven Caney's

Invention
B·O·O·K

From inspiration to prototype, everything you need to know. Featuring easy at-home projects to start now, plus 35 Great American Invention Stories.

The zipper— 50 years in the making.

America's most delicious accident.

Roller skates, from the ballroom to the playground.

Workman Publishing Co. 1985

TRY YOUR HAND AS AN INVENTOR!

Inventing Rube Goldberg Style

Use any six action components to create an imaginative Rube Goldberg style sequential design invention for these ideas:

Automatic Fanning Machine For Hot Days

Bedroom Burglar Alarm

Remote Control TV Channel Changer

Around the Block Dog Walker

Garbage Disposal Device

Your Own Invention Idea

SUB SANDWICH   WILD CARD   FAN   FALSE TEETH   STRING   WATER CAN

A Better Mousetrap

Mouse comes out of hiding for submarine sandwich (bait) left on counter. Mouse follows line of bread crumbs. Mouse walks into path of fan and is blown across counter... into false teeth. Teeth clamp shut to hold mouse... also pulling a string... which tilts water can to drown mouse.

CAT   ICE CUBES   CHAMPAGNE   MATCHES   CUCKOO CLOCK   PIGEON

CANNON   HORN   SPRINGBOARD   BUCKET   SAW   TEA KETTLE

BALLOON   WEIGHT   CANDLE   FROG   MAGNET   UMBRELLA

Page 38 reprinted with permission of Workman Publishing Co. ☉ 1985

BECOME AN INVENTOR: APPLY FLEXIBLE THINKING!

Inventors look at things that people need and by bringing elements together in new ways, find ways to meet these needs. Look at the items pictured below. Combine these items, using as many as you can to invent:

A HOUSEHOLD BURGLAR ALARM	A METHOD FOR WATERING PLANTS WHILE GONE FROM HOME	A SURE WAY TO GET JOHN TO PRACTICE HIS OBOE

Box of Tacks   **Large Balloon**   **Dog**   **Spider**   **Can Green Beans / Candy Bar**

   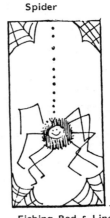 

Bat and Ball   **Alarm Clock**   **Toy Snake**   **Fishing Rod & Line**   **Empty Box**

Large Sandwich   **Tape Recorder**   **Detergent**   **Hot Dog & Bun**   **Colt Pistol**

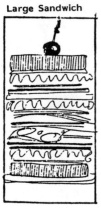 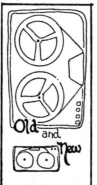 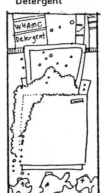   

46

THE HOW-TO BOOK

<u>Lights!</u> <u>Camera!</u> <u>Action!</u>
How A Movie Is Made
  by Gail Gibbons
  Thomas Y. Crowell 1985

Here is a simple but accurate account of the making of a motion picture told in spare text and detailed drawings.

EXAMPLE

I. How A Movie Is Made

   A. Selecting the script

   B. Pre-production
     1. script
     2. cast
     3. location
     4. scenery
     5. costumes
     6. sound-photography
     7. rehearsals

   C. Production
     1. lights
     2. camera
     3. action

   D. Post-production
     1. editing
     2. music
     3. printing
     4. releasing

Writing the How-To Book

STEPS

I. Select A Topic

II. Research and outline the topic

   A. Steps in the how-to process

   B. People involved

   C. Materials needed

   D. Location

   E. Preparatory steps

   F. Production steps

   G. Post-production activities

A HOW-TO MODEL

How I Trained My Colt
By Sandy Rabinowitz
Doubleday, 1980

This is a story about a young girl who trains her colt named Sunny. The book begins with the birth of the colt. The young girl begins working with the animal almost immediately. The girl said, "I wanted to ride him when he grew up. So he had to learn to obey me. He was only two days old. I was bigger and stronger than he was. It was time for Sunny's first lesson."

This book takes the reader from the time the colt was born until he was trained for riding. Each step of the training is carefully described.

Animal Training

Almost any animal can be trained to perform in some way.

Training procedures differ for each animal.

The library has many books on animal training.

Some circus performers train animals.

Some animal trainers work for large zoos.

Obedience schools train animals also.

Creative Reporting

1. Check several resources for information regarding the training of one type of animal.

2. Provide pictures or drawings of the animal that you have chosen.

3. Using the model above develop an instruction manual for training your animal.

4. Decide where the best place would be for the training to take place.

5. Be sure to mention in your story what you hope to accomplish with this training.

Possible choices

hamster	elephant	dog
guinea pig	goldfish	bird
rabbit	monkey	

HOW TO DIG A HOLE
TO THE OTHER SIDE
OF THE WORLD

By Faith McNulty
Harper & Row, 1979

One would have to dig 8,000 miles to reach the other side of the earth. Use a shovel and start digging in a soft place. Loam is the first layer of the earth, which is made of tiny bits of rock mixed with many other things such as plants and worms that died and rotted long ago. In your dig you may hit boiling water or steam that comes from the center of the earth. Stay out of the geysers which may carry you to the surface and shoot you into the air. Find out what causes volcanoes as you journey through this book.

Use this model to prepare a booklet of your journey to the bottom of the ocean. Tell about the animals you might meet along the way to the bottom. What gear would you use to get down to the bottom of the of the ocean? Tell the dangers of the ocean as they did in this book.

What to do:

1. Read all factual material about the ocean.

2. You are the main character so write in the first person (I).

3. Include charts and illustrations in your booklet.

THINGS TO DO WITH WATER

by Illa Podendorf
Childrens Press, 1971

As a liquid water can be made into many different shapes, a circle, a square, etc. By using food colors water can virtually become any color, red, blue, or yellow. By mixing two different colors the water can create a new color such as purple, mixed from red and blue. Water can be evaporated into the air. Experiments with water can be fun and unpredictable. Try these simple experiments in your home. Do you get the same results?

Using this as a model try experimenting with other objects and record the results.

Possible objects to experiment with:

ice	play-doh
wood	clay
air	dirt
magnets	sand
sugar	

What to do:

1. Pick an object to experiment with.

2. Do four experiments as in the book.

3. Describe the experiment in your book.

4. Put the results of your experiment after the explanation.

HOW A HOUSE HAPPENS

By Jan Adkins
Walker and Company, 1972

When building a house one must go through certain steps. One must decide what kind of house is needed (how big, where the rooms should be placed, how many doors and windows, etc.). When a site is picked for the house, the architect can draw up a blueprint or a plan of the house. After the blueprint is finished the contractor and the workmen can start building the house. This book will take you plank by plank through building a house, explaining plumbing, and electrical processes and much more.

Using this model research the way other things are made.

    Possible items to research:

            Automobile assembly line

            How a computer is built

What to do:

1. Research your subject.

2. Write a step by step description of the process, the people who work with developing the item and the parts used.

3. Include diagrams.

Vitamins—
What They Are,
What They Do

JUDITH S. SEIXAS
Illustrated by TOM HUFFMAN

With the same clarity and straightforward presentation that distinguished her highly regarded books on alcohol and tobacco, Judith S. Seixas introduces young readers to vitamins. What vitamins are, how they were discovered, how they work, and whether or not they are safe are some of the topics covered. A complex subject at once made understandable and interesting. Included are a vitamin chart and a true/false test for readers.

Greenwillow Books 1986

Following the pattern of this informational book, select another topic and tell WHAT IT IS and WHAT IT DOES.

Include in your illustrated book:

What is it.

How it was discovered or invented.

How it works.

How safe it is.

A chart or graph.

Diagrams as needed.

A quiz for your reader at the end of the book.

RE/USES

2133 Ways to RECYCLE and REUSE the Things You Ordinarily Throw Away

CAROLYN JABS

Line drawings by Robert Duffek
Crown Publishers, Inc. 1982

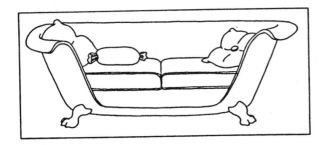

RE-USES is a book about being smart by using what you already have.

It speaks to beating the high cost of living by making more and buying less.

RE-USES recognizes that few people individually can use all the trash they produce. It helps you find out who can use your discards...and perhaps pay you for them.

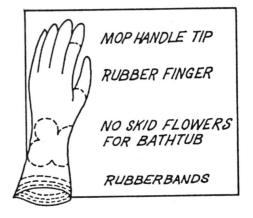

MOP HANDLE TIP

RUBBER FINGER

NO SKID FLOWERS FOR BATHTUB

RUBBER BANDS

FIND OUT!

WHAT IS WASTED OR THROWN AWAY EACH DAY IN YOUR SCHOOL?

HOW COULD IT BE USED?

1. IDENTIFY SOURCES OF WASTE MATERIAL AND POSSIBLE USES OF THIS MATERIAL.
2. MAKE A PLAN FOR MANUFACTURING A USEFUL PRODUCT.
3. RESEARCH SOURCES OF LOANS FOR START UP MONEY.
4. PLAN HOW TO PRODUCE, PACKAGE, AND MARKET THE PRODUCT.
5. INVESTIGATE GOVERNMENT REGULATIONS FOR SMALL BUSINESSES.

MAKE YOUR PRODUCT!

PRODUCTS REQUIRING FLEXIBLE THINKING

RECYCLE YOUR SCHOOL ! ! !

FROM BOTTLE CAPS YOU CAN MAKE

SHOE SCRAPER
GAMES
TAMBOURINE
WASHERS
FISH SCALE SCRAPER
BUTTONS

FROM OLD FORKS YOU CAN MAKE

MINI RAKES
DECORATOR FORKS
MONEY FORK
BRACELET

FROM PLASTIC MEAL OR SERVING
TRAYS YOU CAN MAKE

PAPER PLATES
DRIP CATCHERS
STENCIL PATTERNS
SHOE CUSHIONS
INSULATION FOR SHOES
ARTIST PALETTE
ANTI BOOK SLIPPER
ANTI RUG SLIPPER

WHAT COULD YOU DO WITH

OLD RECORDS
OLD NEWSPAPERS
TOOTHPASTE TUBES
PENCIL SHAVINGS
WASTE PAPER
ORANGE PEELS

HOW WILL YOU MANUFACTURE YOUR PRODUCT ?
WHERE CAN YOU GET A LOAN FOR "START UP" MONEY?

HOW WILL YOU PACKAGE, MARKET AND SELL YOUR PRODUCT?

WHAT BUSINESS REGULATIONS WILL YOU NEED TO FOLLOW?

SO YOU DON'T LIKE TO WRITE!!!!!

TRY: THE NEWSPAPER CLIPPING REPORT

SELECT A TOPIC. This can be on a current event or on a general topic. Here are topics to think about:

AIRCRAFT

BUSINESS

CONSERVATION

DISASTERS

EARTH-OUR-HOME

FUNNY HAPPENINGS

GREAT PERFORMANCES

HUMAN INTEREST STORIES

INTERESTING PEOPLE

JOYFUL MOMENTS

KEEPERS OF FREEDOM

LAW AND ORDER

MISUNDERSTANDINGS

NEW IDEAS

OLYMPIC GAMES

PROPAGANDA

QUASARS

RECORD-SETTING EVENTS

SPACE

TECHNOLOGY

UNUSUAL EVENTS

VICTORIES

WATER

X RAYS AND OTHER
     MEDICAL MIRACLES

YOUTHFUL
     ACCOMPLISHMENTS

ZEALOTS

STEP TWO:

Make a list of all the possible things you might look for and clip as you begin your report.

Here are some topic ideas to get your thinking started.

KEEPERS OF FREEDOM!

How quickly can you find in a newspaper--- add other items

1. A picture that symbolizes freedom
2. A patriotic headline
3. An article about loss of freedom
4. An event that could take place only in a free society
5. A statement concerning freedom of speech
6. A controversial topic
7. The name of one who can do something about injustice
8. The name or picture of a female leader
9.
10.
11.
12.
13.
14.
15.
16.
17.
18.
19.
20.

NEWSPAPER HUNT

CONSERVATION

Find a picture, name or acticle about---add other items

1. A natural resource that is not wildlife
2. A major water source
3. Something that needs to be conserved
4. A product good for the environment
5. Good advice for saving something
6. Someone to write to about a conservation problem
7. Something currently being rehabilitated
8.
9.
10.
11.
12.
13.
14.
15.

TECHNOLOGY

Find a picture, name or acticle about---add other items

1. An energy producer
2. Something a computer expert might use
3. An invention to use in your home
4. An industry that might pollute
5. An example of mass transportation
6. Someone to write about an environmental concern
7. A product that might pollute
8. Someone's opinion of technology
9. A technological job opening
10. Technology in the kitchen
11. Third world technology
12.
13.
14.
15.

THE NEWSPAPER CLIPPING REPORT

PUTTING IT ALL TOGETHER!

WATCH YOUR NEWSPAPER FOR ADS,

PHOTOGRAPHS, CARTOONS   AND

FEATURES RELATED TO THE SUBJECT

YOU CHOOSE.

BEGIN CLIPPING!

SORT YOUR CLIPPINGS INTO MAJOR

SUBJECT HEADINGS...THIS CAN BE

BY DATE OR BY TYPE OF FEATURE

OR OTHER HEADINGS YOU CHOOSE.

DISPLAY FOR OTHERS TO SEE:

    IN A BOOK

    ON THE BULLETIN BOARD

    OR OTHER DISPLAY

REPORTING

WITH A CAMERA,

PAINTS AND

PENCIL

THE ILLUSTRATED OR PHOTOGRAPHIC ESSAY

Use your camera or your sketchpad to record in visual form a series of happenings or events. This means of recording information is particularly effective in showing changes in nature. For example, if you select a place you often see (perhaps your back yard) and begin a series of photos you can show changes in nature and seasons very effectively.

RESEARCHING AND REPORTING

WITH A CAMERA

What a great idea to select one element of nature and pursue it with your camera! You will need to keep a sharp eye out to get just the photographs that will show clearly the one thing in nature that you want others to see. In these books, Jill Bailey photographs parts of animals to test the very young reader's powers of observation and identification.

What element(s) of nature might YOU photograph first in part and then as a whole? By doing this you will create a guessing game book for others to enjoy.

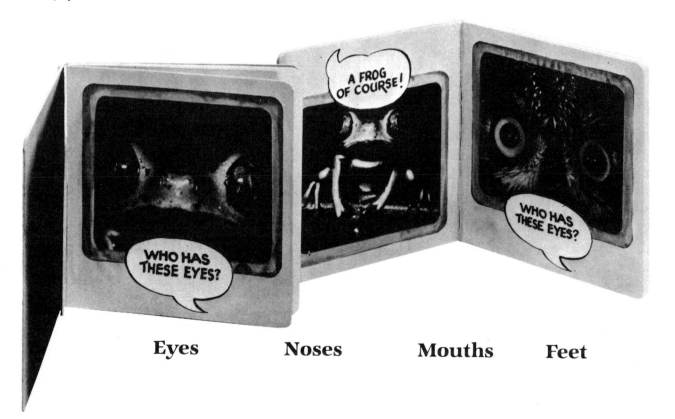

Eyes   **Noses**   **Mouths**   **Feet**

Illustrations from ANIMALS OF COURSE: MOUTHS, NOSES, FEET, EYES by Jill Bailey. Putnam Publishers, 1985

OBSERVING AN ANIMAL

Kitten Can
By Bruce McMillan
Lothrop, Lee, Shepard, 1984

This book is a book full of verbs. The verbs describe the actions of Kitten. The pictures also tell the story of what the kitten does. This is one active animal. It sniffs, climbs, stalks, and springs.

Kittens are very active animals.
There are many other animals that are active and there are some animals that are not as active.
The library has many books about animals.
Observation of an animal can also be useful in developing a story about animals.

Things to search for:
How the animal moves.
How the animal eats.
How the animal plays.
How the animal uses his senses.
Any other interesting traits the animal possesses.
Example:
"Kitten can stare, squeeze, stretch, and scratch."

What to do:

1. Check several sources for information regarding the animal of your choice.

2. List all the action verbs you can find that pertain to your animal.

3. Using the model above, create a story about an animal and be sure to provide illustrations. (replace the word kitten with the name of your animal)

THE PICTORIAL JOURNAL

Here is the story of one family facing all of the dangers and hardships in moving west. Accurate information, cartoon-style illustrations and a first person narrative make this a most exciting real-life tale.

WHAT EVENT FROM HISTORY WILL YOU SELECT TO RESEARCH?

FROM WHOSE VIEWPOINT WILL YOU TELL THE EVENT?

WHAT WILL HAPPEN TO YOUR NARRATOR AT THE END OF YOUR STORY?

NOTE THE IMPORTANCE OF DETAILS IN RECREATING A PARTICULAR TIME OR PLACE. WHAT DETAILS WILL BE IMPORTANT TO YOUR STORY?

REMEMBER, A PICTURE CAN TELL THE STORY! YOUR CAPTIONS UNDER EACH PICTURE SHOULD ADD TO THE STORY (Not tell what is in the picture).

GOING WEST

STORY BY **Martin WADDELL**

Ma

Pa

Kate

PICTURES BY **Philippe DUPASQUIER**

Peter

Louisa

© 1984
Harper & Row, Publishers

POSSIBLE JOURNEYS FOR RESEARCH

TRAVELING TO THE NEW WORLD WITH COLUMBUS

A JEWISH FAMILY ESCAPING FROM GERMANY IN 1939

THE FIRST ASTRONAUTS TO TRAVEL TO THE MOON

TRAVELING TO CHINA WITH MARCO POLO, OR TRAVELING WITH A FAMOUS EXPLORER.

LIFE ON THE SANTA FE TRAIL OR THE OREGON TRAIL

RIDING A BICYCLE ACROSS THE UNITED STATES OR CANADA

TRAVELING DOWN THE MISSISSIPPI RIVER WITH MARK TWAIN

RESEARCHING COMMUNITY CHURCHES

Ashley Wolff, in writing and illustrating The Bells of London, chose one small part of that large, busy city to tell about in pictures and verse. For each church featured in the book there is a rhyming couplet.

"Oranges and lemons,
Say the bells of St. Clements."

Play with words!
What might these bells sing?

St. Johns

St. Annes

St. Martins

Old Bailey

Shoreditch

Stepney

Bow

St. Peters

St. Giles

White Chapel

St. Margarets

Aldgate

St. Catherines

Dodd Mead, 1985

1. How many churches in your community have bells?

2. Make a list of the churches and their locations.

3. Write to each church for a picture of the church (or take pictures of those nearest you).

4. Compose a rhyming couplet telling of what the bells of each church might sing.

5. Put your work in booklet form to share with others.

THE OPTICAL ILLUSION BOOK

SEYMOUR SIMON

Illustrated with drawings and photographs

Praised as "fascinating" (Horn Book) and "extraordinary" (Appraisal), this classic book on optical illusions is *now in paperback!* Readers will discover: why two lines can look uneven when both are really the same length; how perspective creates three-dimensional images; the ways color and brightness influence perception; how artists use illusions to create new vistas. Over 80 illustrations and many fun visual experiments let readers *see* how and why these illusions work. Proving that you can't always believe what you see, this book is sure to open young people's eyes.

Morrow Junior Books 1984

FOOLING FOLKS WITH PHOTOGRAPHS

This book shows that even though we might all look at the same scene or picture, we do not necessarily see the same thing.

Use this idea as a basis for a photographic or a multi- picture research project. You can use a series of unrelated photographs or you might want to use photos all on one topic.

Each photo you include can be captioned to ask the viewer for a response. For example: you might show part of an object and ask the viewer to identify the object.

OR

You might show people engaged in an unusual occupation or event and ask the reader what or why they are doing what they are doing. Explain the real reason on the next page!

OR

Research the works of artists who are well known for the use of optical illusion in their paintings or drawings.

STUDY THE PICTURE BOOKS OF MITSUMASA ANNO

In his books, ANNO'S JOURNEY, ANNO'S ITALY, ANNO'S BRITAIN and ANNO'S U.S.A., this artist uses many optical illusion tricks! Make a list of all those you find and share them with your friends.

OR

Prepare a photographic display of as many optical illusions as you can find. These can be photographs you take or photographs you find in newspapers or magazines.

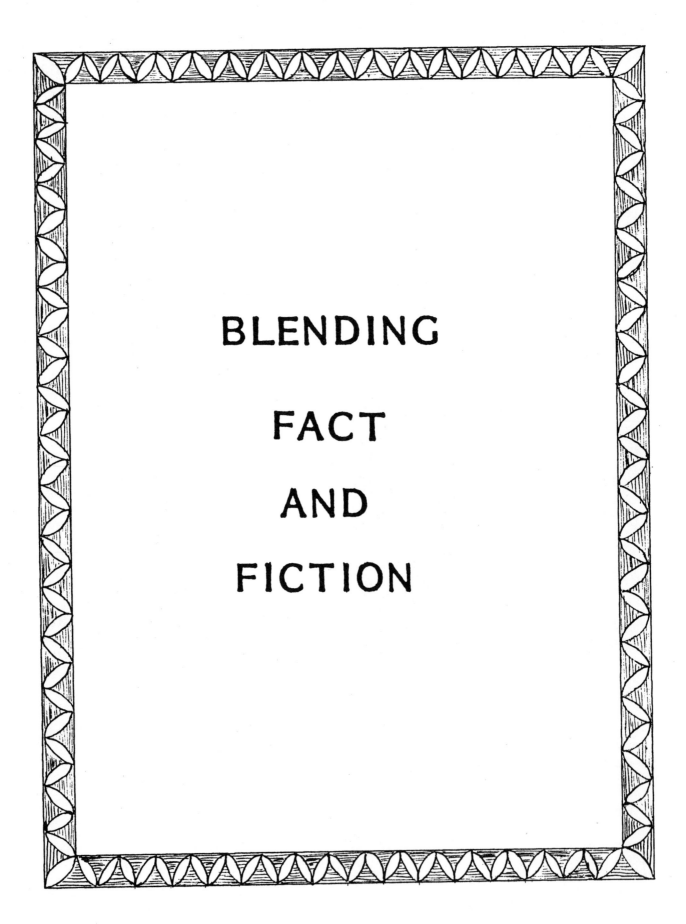

BLENDING

FACT

AND

FICTION

The Emperor's New Clothes

by Hans Christian Anderson   Little Brown
Retold and illustrated by Nadine Westcott   1985

In this tale an Emperor is fooled by two crafty tailors into believing that his suit of invisible cloth can only be seen by SPECIAL PEOPLE until a small boy in the crowd shouts out the truth, "He doesn't have any clothes on!"

All folk tales reveal something about the country or culture from which they come. Use the chart below to compare your culture with that shown in a favorite tale.

CULTURE COMPARISON CHART

Title of Folktale _____

Elements of Culture		Folktale Culture	Your Culture
Most popular means of transportation			
Most popular medium for information			
Most popular music			
Most respected profession(s)			
Role of male	Active? Passive?		
Role of female	Involved? Onlooker? Assertive? Submissive?		

This tale is set in _____ century _____ .

country

WRITER'S BLOCK

Written and illustrated by
MARSHA BAKER

Printed in USA

Book Lures Inc.

USING CARTOONS IN WRITING THE HOW-TO BOOK

In this example the author has used cartoons to explain how to start writing when you don't have any ideas. While the cartoons are humorous, good advice is found in the story. Use this idea to write an advice or a how-to book after carefully researching the topic you choose.

WRITER'S BLOCK IS ONE OF THE MOST DREADED DISEASES KNOWN TO MAN

HOWEVER, DO NOT DESPAIR! THE EXPERTS HAVE GOTTEN TOGETHER TO COME UP WITH A CURE FOR WRITER'S BLOCK.

DO YOU HAVE A LOT ON YOUR MIND?

TAKE A LOAD OFF.

RELAX! TAKE A WHOLE WEEK OFF

DON'T BE CHAINED TO HABIT

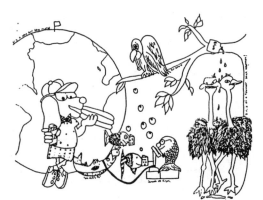

STRETCH YOUR MIND! READ ABOUT NEW AND INTERESTING THINGS

LET YOUR IMAGINATION RUN WILD

AFTER THIS WRITER'S BLOCK WILL BE GONE AND YOU WILL BE WRITING ONCE AGAIN!

Jane R. Howard
WHEN I'M SLEEPY
illustrated by Lynne Cherry

E. P. Dutton 1985

With magnificent illustrations and spare text, this author-artist team shows the sleeping animal world by placing a young child in its center. A careful look at the illustrations will reveal considerable information about animal habitats.

Using a format similar to this book can you show with simple text and illustrations one of the following:

A. How and where animals eat.
(When I'm Hungry)

B. How and where animals shelter from bad weather.
(When It Storms)

C. How animals keep clean.
(When I'm Hungry)

D. How animals play.
(When I Play)

List the animals you plan to research.

_____   _____   _____

_____   _____   _____

_____   _____   _____

What single aspect of animal life will you research? Eating? Sheltering? Playing? Other _____

The title of your book _____

A STORY REPORT

I MET A POLAR BEAR by Selma and Pauline Boyd
Lothrop, Lee and Shepard, 1983

Here is a story model for reporting research on animal homes. On his way to school a boy meets a polar bear, an earthworm and an ant. In helping each to return to its natural home the boy is late to school.

1. What animals will you decide to meet on your way to school? Name four.

    a) _____   c) _____

    b) _____   d) _____

2. What is the natural home of each animal?

    a) _____   c) _____

    b) _____   d) _____

3. How will you help each animal return to its natural home?

    a) _____

    b) _____

    c) _____

    d) _____

4. Write and illustrate your story. Decide how to explain being late to your teacher.

5. Share your story with friends.

Hello!   Greetings!   Good Morning!

70

The Truth About the Moon

by *CLAYTON BESS*

Illustrated in two colors by ROSEKRANS HOFFMAN

THE TRUTH ABOUT THE MOON by Clayton Bess (Houghton Mifflin, 1983) points up the contrasts between modern and traditional beliefs by combining current scientific knowledge and imaginative folklore.

This book can serve as an excellent model for reporting on the differences between mythological and factual explanations of nature.

DECIDE WHAT TOPIC YOU WOULD LIKE TO TELL THE TRUTH ABOUT!

WHAT LEGENDS OR STORIES EXIST ABOUT THE TOPIC?

READ AND BRIEFLY SUMMARIZE THE LEGENDS.

LOCATE FACUTAL INFORMATION ABOUT THE TOPIC.

WRITE YOUR BOOK ALTERNATING PAGES OF MYTH AND FACTUAL EXPLANATION.

OR

STATE A MYTHOLOGICAL EXPLANATION YOU HAVE FOUND FOR SOME ASPECT

OF NATURE AND ASK YOUR READER WHETHER IT IS FACT OR FICTION.

ON THE PAGE THAT FOLLOWS LET YOUR READER KNOW THE ANSWER

AND GIVE THE SCIENTIFIC EXPLANATION FOR THE EVENT

Possible Titles

The Truth About Tides	The Truth About Roses
The Truth About Comets	The Truth About Skunks
The Truth About Weather	The Truth About _____

PROBLEM-SOLVING

One way an author can tell about real-life problems is to present the problem in story form.

Mrs. Tortino lives in a tiny older home surrounded by tall new buildings. These buildings block out the sun and the busy street traffic pollutes the air. Even though her plants begin to die and her cat begins to wheeze, Mrs. Tortino refuses to move. Instead, she finds a unique way to get back sunshine and fresh air!

CREATE A SOLUTION!

Write a story about a different problem (world hunger, unemployment, crime, noise pollution).

by Shirley and Pat Murphy
Lothrop, Lee & Shepard, 1980

What to do:

1. Read about the topic (problem) you have chosen.

2. List solutions suggested by others.

3. Decide on a main character and how this character is affected by the problem.

4. Plan your solution.

5. Write your story, solving the problem.

6. Illustrate your story if possible.

LYDIA DABCOVICH

Mrs. Huggins and Her Hen Hannah

E.P. Dutton 1985

Using humorous illustrations and a story format, the author/artist shows many of the tasks that must be performed on a farm.

Using this same idea, report on the variety of tasks that are performed on a regular basis if you live

In a lighthouse
At the White House
In a weather station
    at the North Pole

In a firehouse
In a forest ranger's cabin
On a ranch
Other _____

Decide:

1. Who will be the main character in you story?

2. What tasks will the character perform?

3. Who will help the character?

4. What problem will the character or the helper have?

5. How will the problem be solved?

Mousekin Takes A Trip
Prentiss Hall, Inc., 1976
Story and pictures by Edna Miller

A white footed mouse is searching for food. He ventures into a camper trailer and the door shuts behind him. As he is munching on some food the trailer begins to move and mouse is on his way.

The trailer, pulled by a car, travels for a long time and when it stops mouse prepares to escape. As the trailer door opens, mouse springs free and lands right in the middle of a desert.

The sights, sounds, and animals are all new to mouse. He is frightened and alone.

> What did mouse see and hear?
> What animals lived there?
> How did mouse get home?

The story answers all of these questions.

Take an Unexpected Trip

Using the above model, take your reader on an unexpected trip through one of the fifty states. Make your story interesting by including the sights and sounds of the state as was done by the desert trip that mouse took. Don't forget that the climate and topography are also important.

What to do:

1. Read as much as you can on the state you choose.
2. List all points of interest you want to use.
3. Place your locations in a logical order.
4. Choose a small animal as your main character.
5. Be sure to include how he accidentally took this trip.
6. Write your story taking your character to several sights and explain the climate it encounters.
7. Make the ending happy by returning the animal to it's home.
8. Use illustrations when possible.

74

KEEP A DIARY!

A Mouse's Diary
By Michelle Cartlidge
Lothrop, Lee, and Shepard Books, 1981

A mouse keeps a diary for a week telling of the activities he is involved in each day of the week.

Sunday
    I went to the park with my father and mother and younger brother. We had a lovely picnic.

Monday
    At ballet class today we pretended to be candles on a great big birthday cake.

Tuesday
    After school my mother took us to the toy shop.

Using the format of this book, write a diary that a historical person might have kept based on facts you find in your research.

Possible Historical Figures

        Paul Revere during Revolutionary War
        George Washington when crossing the Delaware
        Jim Bowie at the Alamo
        Molly Pitcher during the Revolutionary War
        Sacajawea guiding Lewis and Clark

What to do:

1. Read biographies and autobiographies of the person you have picked.

2. Check history books

3. Compile information in diary form as if you were the historical person (use first person "I").

CONTRASTING LIFESTYLES

Toby In The Country, Toby In The City
By Maxine Zohn Bozzo
Greenwillow Books, 1982

In this book two boys, named Toby lead practically the same lives, except one boy lives in the city and the other boy lives in the country. Toby in the country lives on a farm while Toby in the city lives in an apartment. The street in front of Toby's house in the country is a gravel road bordered with trees. The street in front of Toby's apartment in the city is a busy intersection with a few trees. Toby in the country plays games in the woods with his friends. Toby in the city plays hopscotch on the busy sidewalk with his friends. The two boys do   many of the same things but in different ways because life in the city is different from life in the country.

Use this model to compare and contrast two subjects. Illustrations will be necessary for this project.

Possible items to compare and contrast:

The Indians and the Pilgrims

Two types of dinosaurs

A child in France or Spain to a child in U.S.

What to do:

1. Decide on the two subjects.

2. Research the subjects the library, in an encyclopedia, a social studies book, or a specialty book about your subject.

3. After gathering information needed, write and illustrate your book.

Pancake Pie
SVEN NORDQVIST
EDIBLE ORIGINS: RESEARCHING THE SOURCE OF FOODS WE EAT

Wily Farmer Festus and his exuberant cat Mercury like to make a good thing even better. Three times a year they sit down to a mouth-watering pancake pie and celebrate Mercury's birthday. But one birthday morning, absolutely nothing goes right. Before he can bake the pie, Festus has to fish a key from the bottom of a deep well, wade through a puddle of broken eggs, and outwit an angry bull with fast cat Mercury as matador. With luck, pluck, and wild invention, Festus and Mercury get over, under, and around all obstacles to have their best birthday celebration ever!

Morrow Junior Books, 1985

PANCAKE PIE is a great spoof on finding and using all of the ingredients found in a birthday pie.

This same idea can be used in weaving factual information into a humorous story about securing the ingredients in any recipe!

Remember, the primary source of all foods is the SUN.

Select a recipe. Develop a chart showing how all the ingredients can be traced back to the sun. Use this information in developing a humorous story about preparing this recipe. Decide WHY this recipe is being prepared (what is the important event?). WHO is the recipe being prepared for? WHEN will the dish be served? WHERE will it be served? WHAT will happen during the finding of the ingredients?

REMEMBER: EVERY STORY HAS

CHARACTERS

SETTING

PROBLEM

SOLUTION

AN ALTERNATE FOODS RESEARCH PROJECT

The President of the United States has just informed you that he or she has selected your home as the typical home in your state and plans to come   to dinner.

Plan a menu of the dinner you will serve the President. You may only use foods raised or grown in your state. You may only use ingredients raised or grown in your state.

WHAT WILL YOU SERVE THE PRESIDENT?

DESCRIBING WHAT A THING IS NOT!

The Man Whose Name Was Not Thomas
by M. Jean Craig
Doubleday and Company, Inc. 1981

"The man whose name was not Thomas or Richard either had to earn a living, just as most men do. He was not a blacksmith or a carpenter. He did not weave cloth or mend shoes. He was not a farmer or a bricklayer or a fisherman. He was something else."

Through the following pages this man is described, but not by what he is, but by what he is not.

Use this model to describe an animal.

What to do:

1. Decide on an animal.

2. Read about this animal-compare it to other animals.

3. Describe what it is by what it is not and can not do.

4. Place your information in a logical order.

SAMPLE:

Rover was not a cat. He was not a rabbit either. He was not a turtle, or an ant or a spider. He was not a monkey or rooster or duck. In fact, he was not even a bear. No he was called something else.

Continue to describe your animal by what he does not do, where he does not live, what he does not eat, what he does not like, etc.

Houghton-Mifflin 1978

Suppose that the bulk mail rates were drastically reduced and all bulk mail was released on the same day. Should this happen, the total weight would cause our entire civilization to collapse.

David Macaulay begins Motel of the Mysteries with this assumption.

The book opens in the year 7000 A.D. A group of archaeologists are unearthing the North American civilization of the 1990s. One of the first things found is a motel (which is assumed to be a tomb).

I.   What significance might the scientists give to:

A television set?   A telephone?   A drain stopper?
A shower cap?   A Do Not Disturb sign?

II. Use this same idea to report on a current place or event through the eyes of one from another civilization. Here are some ideas to get you started.

How Would

Orville and Wilber Wright
Alexander the Great
Shakespeare
Florence Nightengale
Marconi

View

A modern airport
A guided missle site
A word processing lab
An intensive care unit
A television studio

THE
LITTLE
WORM
BOOK

Janet & Allan Ahlberg

THE VIKING PRESS   NEW YORK

THE COMMON WORM

All good worms have a beginning, a middle and an end.

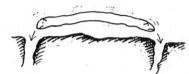

Worms with two beginnings, a middle and no end are apt to injure themselves.

Worms with two ends, a middle and no beginning get bored.

THE

FIVE CHAPTER

BOOK

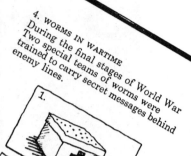

4. WORMS IN WARTIME
During the final stages of World War Two special teams of worms were trained to carry secret messages behind enemy lines.

1.

2.

3. RUN FOR IT

Viking Press 1979

In this spoof on the formal research paper, the Ahlbergs have presented a topic in five chapters.
THE TOPIC IS WORMS!

They have called their paper THE LITTLE WORM BOOK

Contents:

CHAPTER ONE: THE COMMON WORM

CHAPTER TWO: YOU AND YOUR WORM

CHAPTER THREE: WORMS AROUND THE WORLD

CHAPTER FOUR: A SHORT HISTORY OF THE WORM

CHAPTER FIVE: WORMS OF CHARACTER

Select a topic of interest to you. Read this model carefully. Note how the authors make the absurd seem plausible!

What chapters might you have on your topic?

Illustrations will help in your spoof as they do in the Ahlbergs' book!

The Tin-Pot Foreign General and the Old Iron Woman

A stunning anti-war statement!

by Raymond Briggs
illustrated in full color and black and white by the author

Raymond Briggs, author of the critically acclaimed book, *When the Wind Blows,* has written another provocative anti-war statement. In both art and text, this book evokes the mania, futility, and senseless horrors of war. This particular story is about the Falkland Islands War, but the statement Mr. Briggs makes is much more far-reaching and concerns the broader ramifications of man's inhumanity to man as exercised in the deadliest power game of all—WAR!

HISTORY AS SATIRE

Satire: An artistic work that attacks human vice or foolishness with irony, derision or wit.

In this satire the author chooses a recent historical event, the Falkland Islands War and through gross exaggeration shows the foolishness of this or any other conflict between human beings.

1)   Study Briggs' technique as demonstrated in this work.
2)   Select another incident from recent or past history.
3)   Decide how you can exaggerate the incident to present your message.

EXAMPLES

Suppose Chicken Little were concerned with nuclear fallout.
What if the country mouse visited the city mouse at the White House?
How would JACK AND THE BEANSTALK be different if Jack's mother received an allotment for NOT growing beans?
Suppose the THREE BILLY GOATS GRUFF were trying to cross the Berlin Wall.

THE TIN POT FOREIGN GENERAL AND THE OLD IRON WOMAN is published by Little-Brown Publishers, 1985.

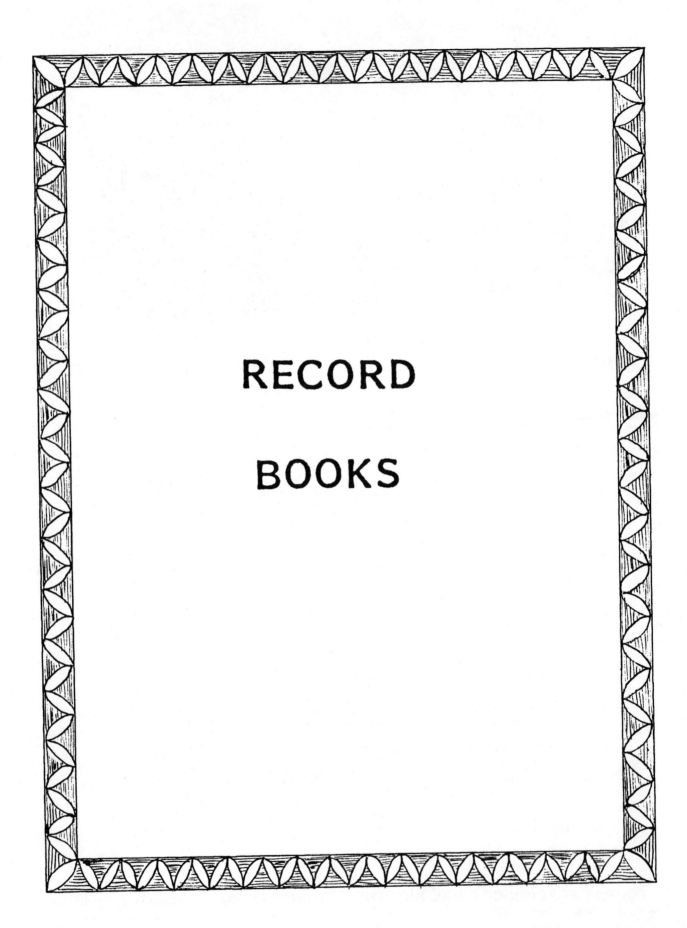

RECORD

BOOKS

A BOOK OF
    AVERAGES!

Here is a book about things that
<u>usually</u> happen each day in the
United States. From this book you
can discover:

How many American teenagers
receive allowances.

How much the average American
family watches television.

How many Americans order
hamburgers, steaks or other items
as their favorite restaurant food.

and hundreds of other facts.

The "Average American" Book

How happy we are • How honest we are • How often we have sex •
Our musical tastes • How often we go to McDonald's •
How much we drink • How much television our kids watch •
How many of us commit adultery

WHAT THE LATEST SURVEYS,
POLLS AND LIFESTYLE STUDIES
TELL US ABOUT THE NOT VERY
AVERAGE AMERICAN PEOPLE.

Compiled and Edited
Barry Tarshis

Atheneum, 1979

A CLASS PROJECT

IN ONE DAY AT _____ School.

Compile a book of statistics about your school. It is sure to be a best
seller! Gather statistics from the library, office, nurse, custodian, other
classrooms, and bus drivers. Keep records for two weeks and average your
figures to arrive at a statistic. Brainstorm with friends concerning items to
research. Here are starters.

1. How many pencils are sharpened in your school each day?

2. How many students (or teachers) are late each day?

3. How many lunches are served?

4. How many band-aids are used?

   KEEP GOING!

Here is a collection of truly appalling decisions! Notable bad decisions covered include:

° the famous firm that turned down the patent for the typewriter, safe in the knowledge that "No mere machine can replace an honest and reliable clerk."

° the German technical institute that refused admittance to young Albert Einstein because "he showed no promise."

° the literature professor who gave a 0 in composition to one of his pupils – Emile Zola.

° the twenty-one publishers who turned down M.A.S.H.

YOUR PROJECT:
The Worst Decisions of

Our Town
Our School
Our Class.

DAVID FROST'S BOOK OF THE WORLD'S WORST ~~DECISIONS~~ DESISIONS

by David Frost and Michael Deakin
illustrated by Arnie Levin

Crown Publishers 1983

1. Select the group you want to survey.

2. Consider convincing arguments to convince those you interview to share their worst decisions for publication.

3. Compile and categorize your data.

4. Write your book!

Would You Believe This, Too?
More Useless Information You
Can't Afford To Be Without
By Deidre Sanders
Illustrated by Joyce Behr
Sterling Publishing Co., Inc. 1976

Would You Believe This, Too? is a collection of strange facts. This book is filled with information about people, plants, animals, history, science, literature, business, industry, agriculture, and sports.

"Scaled up to size and speed, the common house spider could give a world champion sprinter eight seconds start in a 100-meter race and still beat him."

A fact is information that is really true. Some facts are so strange that they are hard to believe.

Sometimes people believe information that is not true. These beliefs or customs are called superstitions. Sometimes these sayings are also called wive's tales.

Use this model as a way of reporting research about superstitions, old sayings, and wive's tales.

Directions to follow

1. Collect as many sayings, superstitions, and old wive's tales as you can find.

2. Construct a book. Each page should contain one or two sayings.

3. Tell whether the statement is true or false.

4. Illustrate the pages and design a cover for your book.

5. Give your book a title.

WHERE TO SEARCH

Interview as many people as possible. Most people have heard a number of superstitions and will be happy to share them with you.

THE BIG BOOK OF ANIMAL RECORDS

written and illustrated
by Annette Tison
and Talus Taylor

AN
ANIMAL
RECORD
BOOK

Here are all kinds of records set by all kinds of animals! As you read this book, note the <u>kinds</u> of records cited.

From the pygmy shrew weighing less than an ounce to the great blue whale, here are all kinds of animals and facts about which is the largest, the smallest, the fastest, the slowest, and, of course, the strangest and most unusual. Annette Tison, a young French artist and naturalist, and Talus Taylor, an artist and former biology teacher, have collaborated on several popular children's books. For *The Big Book of Animal Records,* they worked on the text and illustrations for two years to convey the information strikingly, accurately, and also humorously.

<u>TO</u> <u>WRITE</u> <u>YOUR</u> <u>BOOK</u>

1) Select a topic. The Big Book of (Insect) (Fish) (Mammal) (Reptile) Records.

2) Decide on the records you will include. List several here.

a) The fastest _____

b) The oldest _____

c) The _____ which sleeps the longest.

d) The _____ with the most _____.

e) _____

3) Research the answers to your questions. Each question and answer can be an illustrated page in your book.

THE BIG BOOK OF ANIMAL RECORDS is published by Grosset & Dunlap, 1985.

AMAZING ACHIEVEMENTS

The Guinness Book of Amazing Achievements by Norris and Ross McWhirter (Sterling Publishing Co., 1974) many amazing things that people have done are recorded. You can read about everything from the longest mustache ever grown to the person with the strongest teeth in the world.

1. Compile a book of amazing achievements of students in your class. Almost anyone has

    > been somewhere
    > done something
    > collects or owns something
    >   or
    > met someone

    that no one else can claim.

2. Ask questions and record the answers.

3. Write and illustrate your book allowing one page for each amazing achievement. Some of your illustrations can be photographs if you have permission of those involved.

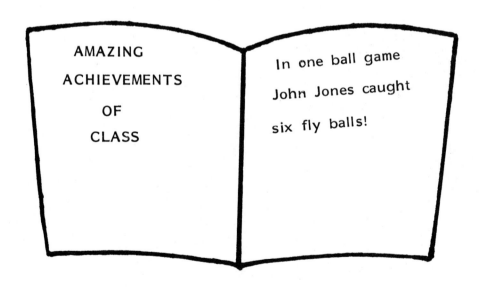

AMAZING
ACHIEVEMENTS
OF
CLASS

In one ball game John Jones caught six fly balls!

RECORD BOOKS!

WHAT'S THE BIGGEST?
by Barbara R. Fogel
Illustrated by Barbara Wolff
Random House, 1966

"What's the Biggest?" explains some surprising facts and theories about bigness in man-made things, in animals and men, on earth and in the universe. The author explores such questions as these: What's the biggest living reptile? What's the biggest building? What's the biggest river?

Scientists search for the biggest living things on the earth, and they investigate things that are increasing in size.

Increase your vocabulary!

You are to conduct a search for the biggest words. Use this model to research and report your findings.

BIGGEST WORDS FROM "A" TO "Z"

to get you started

1. (A) antidisestablishmentarianism
2. (B)
3. (C)
4. (D)
5. (E)
6. (F)
7. (G)
8. (H)
9. (I)
10. (J)
11. (K)
12. (L)
13. (M)

14. (N)
15. (O)
16. (P)
17. (Q)
18. (R)
19. (S)
20. (T)
21. (U)
22. (V)
23. (W)
24. (X)
25. (Y)
26. (Z)

USING MEASUREMENT AS A REPORTING TOOL!

Here is a great research model which gives interesting information in the form of measurement facts. Learn about the longest, tallest, oldest, youngest, and many more measurement facts! Use this model for reporting YOUR research on an interesting topic. You may want to write THE LONGEST BOOK, or THE TALLEST BOOK or perhaps THE OLDEST BOOK! All of the information in your book will have to do with records on the measurement you have selected.

For example: if you choose THE WIDEST BOOK you might include : 1) The widest river in your state. 2) The widest door in your school. 3) The widest country in the world. You can think of many more. Include an illustrated page for each fact you include.

HOW LONG?
To Go, To Grow, To Know
ROSS and PATRICIA OLNEY
Illustrated by R. W. ALLEY

Do you know how long it takes for your finger-nails to grow a half an inch? How long does a giant sequoia tree live? Have you any idea how long it would take to get to the moon—if you had to walk? You'll find out in *How Long?* This easy-to-read book introduces young readers to the important relationship between time and change. Using fascinating comparisons, the simply written text explains that changes occur throughout nature at varying rates.

William Morrow, 1984

A WORD OF ADVICE IN RESEARCHING: DEVELOP VERY SPECIFIC QUESTIONS!

The more specific your question is, the easier it is to find the answer.
For example: If your question is, "What is the longest river?" what
do you really mean? The longest river in the world? The longest in
your state? The longest in North America?

EXAMPLES OF GOOD QUESTIONS

What is the TALLEST building in Chicago?
Who is the HEAVIEST player playing in the National Football League today?
What is the WIDEST river in North America?

ENCYCLOPEDIA BROWN'S BOOK OF WACKY SPIES

DONALD J. SOBOL

Illustrated by TED ENIK

Morrow Junior Books 1984

Encyclopedia Brown is back, with a zany new collection of tales from the madcap world of espionage. Although he's kept pretty busy through the now-famous Brown Detective Agency, Encyclopedia still finds time to gather tales and trivia about wacky spies. Followers of the dauntless young sleuth can once again giggle and gasp over the colorful exploits of spies both inept and ingenious.

A BOOK OF WACKY FACTS!

What a wonderful collection of true but wacky facts about spies throughout history!

Use this model as a way of reporting research about the town or city or state or province in which you live!

Every community has its funny or strange stories. Many of the older residents of the community could tell you of strange and wacky things that have happened over the years.

Your local historical society can provide letters, diaries, and local histories as a source for YOUR book.

Sometimes, public libraries have a local history section where information is available on both the usual and the unusual happenings of the area.

YOU ARE SURE TO HAVE A BEST SELLER!

WHAT TO SEARCH FOR

Search for wacky facts about:

Agriculture (crops. livestock etc.)
Awards, medals
Colleges, universities
Corporations, businesses
Disasters
Discoveries, inventions
Economics
Education
Elections
Famous people

Flags, names, mottos
Landmarks
Laws and documents
Memorable dates'
Meteorological information(weather)
Parks, amusement centers
Population information(changes etc)
Sports
Surveys of resident preferences
Any other topic you discover!

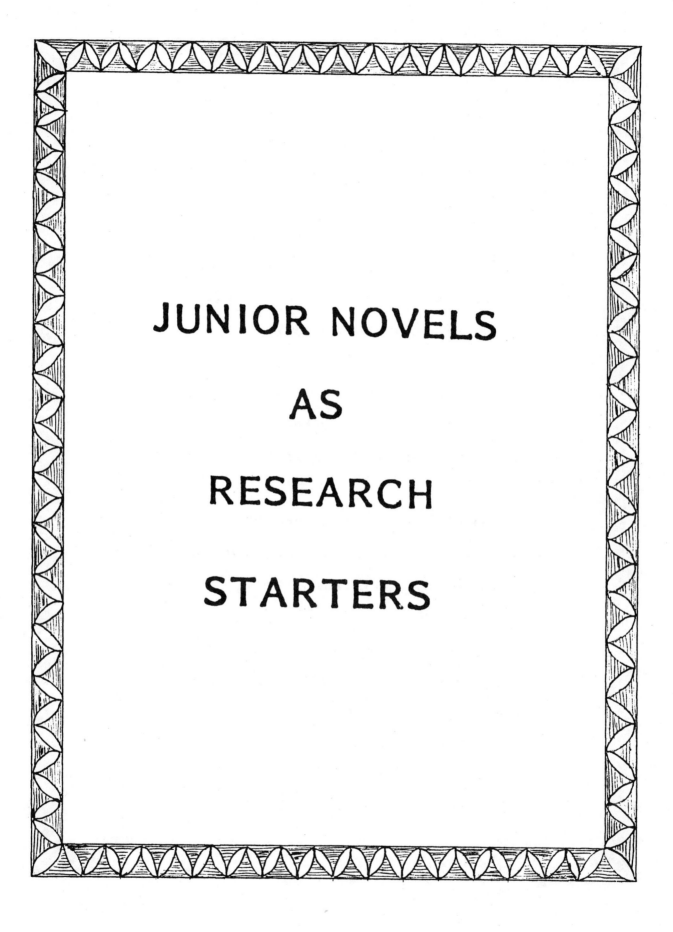

JUNIOR NOVELS

AS

RESEARCH

STARTERS

USING JUNIOR NOVELS

as Springboards to Research

In selecting a particular time period, setting or subject for a junior novel, authors often must do considerable research to assure authentic background for the story.

Students are often turned on to topics of interest through the reading of these carefully researched junior novels.

Found in this section are twenty-six topics, each of which has served as the background for an outstanding junior novel.

Students can carry out the suggested research activities either BEFORE OR AFTER reading the suggested junior novel or another novel on a similar topic.

Research topics are arranged in alphabetical order.

ANIMAL ASSISTANT

Imagine that you own an unusual animal. How could you earn a living by utilizing that animal in a humane way?

1. What animal would you choose? _____

2. List ten traits of that animal:

3. List ten things someone might hire the animal to do:

_____   _____

_____   _____

_____   _____

_____   _____

_____   _____

_____   _____

_____   _____

_____   _____

_____   _____

_____   _____

4. Think of a business that would allow you to use the animal's traits to provide a needed service. Be as original as you can.

_____

5. Write a job description telling what services you and the animal will provide, qualifications for both of you, and what you will charge.

_____

_____

_____

_____

_____

Read Journey to an 800 Number by E. L. Konigsburg (Atheneum, 1983) to find out how Wood Stubbs earns a living with his camel, Ahmed.

BLIND FATE

Imagine that you have discovered that your dog is going blind. The veterinarian says there is no treatment. What problems is your dog likely to have?

_____

_____

_____

_____

How will his behavior change?

_____

_____

Use the grid below to evaluate alternative solutions to the problem.

1 = no 2 = maybe 3 = yes	Is it possible?	Will the dog be in pain?	How will you feel?	Your criteria	TOTAL
Tie him up					
Put him to sleep					
Let him roam free like he used to					
Turn him over to research laboratory					
Other:					

Read <u>The Trouble With Tuck</u> by Theodore Taylor (Doubleday, 1981)

SERENDIPITY SEARCH

You are a counselor at Camp Serendipity. One of the campers has run away. Make a plan for finding the missing camper. The other counselors and the rest of the campers will be glad to help you. How will you organize the search?

1. What steps will you need to take to find the missing camper quickly?

_____

_____

_____

2. What areas of the camp will you need to search?

_____

_____

3. How will you assign the counselors and campers who are willing to help you?

_____

_____

_____

4. What materials or supplies might the search teams need?

_____

_____

5. What problems might arise during the search? What are some possible solutions to those problems?

_____

_____

_____

_____

_____

_____

Read There's A Bat In Bunk Five by Paula Danziger (Delacorte, 1980)

TIC-TAC-TOE WITH DOG FACTS

Complete any three squares down, across, or diagonally. Use the books in the reference area to verify your answers. Identify your source in the square with the answer.

Name a breed suitable for training as a guide dog for the blind.	Tell one technique for training a dog to obey or do a trick.	List five characteristics of a responsible dog owner.
Name and describe one disease against which a dog needs protection.	Name one trait necessary for a guide dog.	What do you consider the most important criteria in choosing which breed of dog is the best pet?
Name one breed suitable for being a sled dog.	What traits and characteristics are vital for a sled dog?	Tell one instance when a dog is credited with saving a human's life.

Source:

Source:

Source:

Source:

Source:

Source:

Read Stone Fox by John Reynolds Gardiner (Thomas Y. Crowell, 1980)
What's One More? by Margaret Poynter (Atheneum, 1985)
The Trouble With Tuck by Theodore Taylor (Doubleday, 1981)

EASE INTO ECONOMICS

Research the terminology of economics, especially the principles on this page. Match these terms with the fictional incidents on the next page that demonstrate what the term means.

A. Incentive and reward system

B. Risk capital

C. Supply and demand

D. Investment in human resources

E. Monopoly

F. Trade-off

G. Diversification

H. Mass Production

I. Risk

J. Price War

K. Advertising

L. Consignment

M. Stock Option

N. Sales Promotion

O. Opportunity cost

Read Millie Willenheimer and the Chestnut Corporation by Dean Hughes
      (Atheneum, 1983)
      Tybee Trimble's Hard Times by Lila Perl (Clarion, 1984)
      Kid Power by Susan Beth Pfeffer (Franklin Watts, 1977)
      Kid Power Strikes Back by Susan Beth Pfeffer (Franklin Watts, 1984)
      No Monsters in the Closet by Willo Davis Roberts (Atheneum, 1983)
      My Horrible Secret by Stephen Roos (Delacorte, 1983)

ECONOMICS

_____ 1. Claire has two money-making projects, while Warren has only one.

_____ 2. Janie was offered a job to walk a Great Dane for $1/day. When she agreed, she forgot that she had made plans to meet her best friend for a movie.

_____ 3. You have to spend money to make money.

_____ 4. The newspaper carrier who gets the most new subscriptions wins a prize.

_____ 5. Mr. Brinker will sell Millie's chestnuts at his drugstore for 35¢ and give her 30¢.

_____ 6. Father has to give up job as a law clerk in order to have time to study for bar exam.

_____ 7. Johnny wanted to be the only person in town providing a snow shoveling service.

_____ 8. It takes too long to make Muscle Milk with just one blender, so the boys call Laurel who comes to help and brings two more blenders.

_____ 9. Millie decides to take Bradley's chestnuts in exchange for shares in the company at a rate of 5¢ each.

_____ 10. Mother gives up regular job at the library to paint rooms for an interior decorator. The pay is better, but there is no guarantee of regular jobs.

_____ 11. Laurel makes posters telling about the barbecue she is having.

_____ 12. Dad says no more allowance, but he will pay 25¢ for each dollar Millie earns on her own.

_____ 13. If Millie owns all the chestnuts in town, she should be able to control the price.

_____ 14. If you charge less, more customers will use your service.

_____ 15. Tybee uses some of the money she had been saving for a circus ticket to buy her mother a plant while she is in the hospital.

YOUR LUCKY DAY!

You have just won a million dollars. It is to be paid $50,000 each year for twenty years. Think of the things you will want during the next twenty years for yourself and your family.

The chart below is divided into five year periods. For each period, tell five things you might do with the money received those years. Rate your ideas according to the criteria listed. Remember what your age will be during those years.

1 = no 2 = maybe 3 = yes IDEAS	Will it be of lasting value?	Will it help other people?	Am I old enough or responsible enough?	Your criteria
Now to five years from now				
Five years to ten years				
Ten years to fifteen years				
Fifteen years to twenty years				

Read Million Dollar Jeans by Ron Roy (Dutton 1983)

TO CATCH A GERBIL

Your mother reluctantly agreed to let you have two gerbils, Romeo and Juliet. Soon you have nine more. You decide not to tell your mother since she dislikes gerbils so much. Then one day Nicky Coletti comes over to visit and lets the gerbils out.

How can you catch them? Design a gerbil trap that will not hurt the prey.

a. Are there any characteristics of gerbils that could help you trap them?

_____

_____

_____

b. What materials could you use as the container to hold the gerbil?

_____

_____

_____

c. What materials could you use to lure the gerbil into the container?

_____

_____

_____

d. Draw a picture of your trap.

Read Anastasia, Ask Your Analyst by Lois Lowry (Houghton Mifflin, 1984)

No ideas? See The Great Hamster Hunt by Lenore and Erik Bleqvad (Harcourt, Brace Jovanovich, 1969)

PROJECT PLANNING

How could you turn one of your hobbies or special interests into a science fair project?

1. List your favorite hobbies or leisure activities:

_____

_____

_____

_____

2. List pets, plants, animals, or insects found around your house:

_____

_____

_____

_____

3. Choose one of these for a science fair project. What will your hypothesis be? What scientific concept will you try to demonstrate?

_____

_____

_____

4. What materials will be needed?

_____

_____

_____

5. What steps will you need to take?

_____

_____

_____

6. What problems might you face?

_____

_____

_____

Read Tough-luck Karen by Johanna Hurwitz (Morrow, 1982)
    Your Former Friend, Matthew by Lou Ann Gaeddert (Dutton, 1984)

COLOR YOUR MOOD

1. Nora can see auras around people. When she sees red around them, they are angry. Green is a good and growing color. She saw an orange aura around her old dog Tolly until the night he died. Her brother's aura is blue. Mr. Cole, her sixth grade teacher, has a yellow aura, usually mixed with blue. Dad's is often gray by the end of the day.

   Think of other colors and what they might mean.

2. List ten people in your life. Tell what color you think their aura would be. Tell why.

People	Color	Reason
1. _____	_____	_____
2. _____	_____	_____
3. _____	_____	_____
4. _____	_____	_____
5. _____	_____	_____
6. _____	_____	_____
7. _____	_____	_____
8. _____	_____	_____
9. _____	_____	_____
10. _____	_____	_____

3. Do you think the aura is based on how a person feels, or does the aura make them feel that way?

   _____

   _____

   _____

   _____

   _____

Read Auras and Other Rainbow Secrets by Lila McGinnis
     (Hastings House 1984)

FOR HIRE

If you were trying to earn money, you might try this suggestion:

1. List ten things you're good at:

_____

_____

_____

_____

_____

_____

_____

_____

2. List ten things someone might need you to do:

_____

_____

_____

_____

_____

_____

_____

_____

3. Think of a business that would allow you to use your skills to provide a needed service. Your business can be something brand-new, something no one else has thought to offer.

_____

4. Write a job description telling what services you will provide, your qualifications, and what you will charge.

_____

_____

_____

_____

_____

Read Anastasia At Your Service by Lois Lowry (Houghton Mifflin, 1982)

PEACEFUL PROTEST

Read about Mohandas K. Gandhi and Martin Luther King. Compare and contrast the lives of these two men.

When and Where he lived:

GANDHI _____

_____

KING _____

_____

Goal in life:

GANDHI _____

_____

KING _____

_____

Means used to pursue this goal:

GANDHI _____

_____

KING _____

_____

Death:

GANDHI _____

KING _____

Awards and Honors:

GANDHI _____

KING _____

Read A Garland for Gandhi by Helen Jacob Pierce (Parnassus, 1968)

Read Martin Luther King Jr: A Man To Remember by Patricia McKissack (Children's Press, 1984)

WHAT'S FOR LUNCH?

If you were alone on an island, and your food supplies were raided by a raccoon, could you survive? Which of the plants below are safe to eat? If the plant is edible, what part should you eat?

1. Red mulberry

2. Huckleberry

3. Papaw

4. Bittersweet

5. Nightshade

6. Mushrooms

7. Clover

8. Nettles

9. Burdock

10. Watercress

11. Marsh marigold (cowslip)

12. Cattail

13. Mistletoe

14. Jerusalem artichoke

15. Arrowhead

16. Chinaberry

Draw a picture of three of the plants that grow in your area of the country which would be safe to eat. Pay careful attention to the shape of leaves or other identifying characteristics.

Read The Island Keeper by Harry Mazer (Delacorte, 1981)

HEROES, HEROINES, AND HISSES

A melodrama is a short play with a heroine who has a problem caused by a mean, nasty villain. Often she owes him money that she cannot pay. He is going to take her land, home, or something of value to fulfill the debt. Finally, a hero arrives to save the day.

The characters in a melodrama have names that fit their role. For instance, you can read about the diabolical plan of Miss Slighcarp and Mr. Grimshaw in The Wolves of Willoughby Chase by Joan Aiken (Doubleday, 1962) or read By The Great Horn Spoon by Sid Fleischman (Little, Brown, 1963) to see how Praiseworthy saves Aunt Arabella. Read Fifth Grade Magic by Beatrice Gormley (Dutton, 1982) to find out about Cadmun Blackheart and Polly Winsum.

1. Use a thesaurus to find words that might be used to describe a character in trouble. Melodramas usually have a pretty young girl as the victim, so you might search for synonyms for such a character.

   _____

   _____

2. Research words that would describe a cold-hearted villain.

   _____

   _____

3. List words that would describe a hero or heroine who is brave and pure of heart.

   _____

   _____

   _____

4. Choose from the descriptive words you have listed to create several possible names for the following characters. They can all be either male or female.

   a. Person in trouble

   b. Villain

   c. Hero or heroine

NAMES AND NOSTALGIA

1. Enid Irene Crowley hates her name. In <u>Taking Care of Terrific</u> by Lois Lowry (Houghton Mifflin, 1983), she says:

> Maybe you have never noticed, but the most hideous adjectives ends in the letter <u>d</u>. Pick up any one of Stephen King's horror novels and open to any page; you'll find them: horrid, putrid, sordid, acrid, viscid, squalid. And the very worse: <u>fetid</u>.

A. Write your first name: _____

B. List ten adjectives ending in the same letter that would describe something bad or negative:

_____   _____
_____   _____
_____   _____
_____   _____
_____   _____

C. List ten good or positive adjectives ending in the same letter as your name:

_____   _____
_____   _____
_____   _____
_____   _____
_____   _____

2. Enid meets several grownups in Boston's Public Gardens who associate root beer with their childhood.

A. Ask a parent or other adult the age of your parents to tell you their five favorite memories of childhood. List them here:

_____
_____
_____
_____
_____

B. Ask a grandparent or someone that age:

_____
_____
_____

C. What do you think your five favorite memories will be when you grow up?

_____
_____
_____

HONORABLE MENTION

1. Imagine that you had the opportunity to be listed in the Guinness Book of World Records for pitching the most games ever won in a row in the history of Little League Baseball.

   a. What would be the advantages of this honor?

   b. What would be the disadvantages?

2. Imagine that you were chosen by the National Kitty Fritters Television Contest as the winner of a cash prize and a chance to appear in a commercial.

   a. What would be the advantages of this honor?

   b. What would be the disadvantages?

3. Which of the two honors described above would you prefer? Give reasons for your answer.

4. If you could achieve your choice of accomplishments that might get you a listing in the Guinness Book of World Records, what would you choose? Why?

Read Skinnybones by Barbara Park (Alfred A. Knopf, 1982)

CONFUCIUS SAY....

Confucius was a Chinese philosopher who probably lived 551-479 B.C. He was, therefore, included in the report Hobie Hanson made to the class on China in Thirteen Ways to Sink a Sub by Jamie Gilson (Lothrop, Lee and Shepard, 1982)

One of Confucius' wise sayings is hidden in each of the puzzles below. Start with the circled letter and move one letter at a time in any direction. You may move diagonally, up, down, or sideways, but you cannot use any circle more than once.

```
E M (T) C A          _____
R O H E U
C R D T I            _____
A M L S O
O E E S U            _____
```

What does this saying mean to you?

_____

_____


```
B O C H T U S
U Y (W) A Y O D      _____
S R O T M O T
E F E D N O W        _____
L D N O T N A
O O O T O S R        _____
N T D O T H E
```

What does this saying mean to you?

_____

_____

109

POWERFUL QUESTIONS

1. Where is the nuclear reactor closest to your home? How far is it?

2. What is the purpose of the cooling water circulating through the core of a nuclear reactor?

3. What is LOCA?

   What are some possible causes?

4. What is meltdown?

5. What is ECCS?

6. What is meant by "the possibility of human error"?

7. What major event occurred in Harrisburg, Pennsylvania on March 28, 1979?

8. Do you believe that Three-Mile Island came within 30-60 minutes of meltdown, and therefore proved nuclear reactors are unsafe?
   Or do you believe that Three-Mile Island proved that the safety systems are effective?

   Give reasons for your opinion?

9. What building materials are used in a containment building?

10. Evacuation plans should exist for what radius around a nuclear plant?

    What problems could arise during evacuation?

11. What government agency is responsible for checking the safety of nuclear power plants?

12. What is the Rasmussen report?

13. What nuclear fuel is used by reactors?

14. What do the control rods do?

15. Is nuclear power worth the risks involved in producing it? State your opinion and the reasons for your decision:

Read Nuclear Energy at the Crossroads by Irene Kiefer (Atheneum, 1982)
      The Nuclear Question by Ann E. Weiss (Harcourt, Brace Jovanovich, 1983)

TICK PICKS AND TICKLE PICKLES

A tick pick is a pair of rhyming one-syllable words that fit a given definition. For instance, a stream in a Balkan country is a Greek creek.

A tickle pickle is a pair of two-syllable rhyming words: a fainter twinkling light is a dimmer glimmer.

Use a dictionary, rhyming dictionary, or thesaurus to solve the following word puzzles.

Tick Picks

1. Colorless crustacean
2. Green cutting instrument
3. Lip caress in Alpine country
4. Search for smallest of litter
5. Man in charge of purchasing
6. Washed legume

Tickle Pickles

1. Out-of-shape feline
2. Lavendar varnish
3. Russian assault
4. Rodent with broad flat tail who makes cloth on a loom
5. Leaping insect's token of admission
6. Hushed eating routine
7. Easy facial indentation
8. Clever cat
9. Overweight male spouse
10. Dark blue sauce for potatoes

DARK DAYS IN THE DOGHOUSE

In The World's Greatest Expert on Absolutely Everything...Is Crying by Barbara Bottner (Harper, 1984), Tucker is inventing a solar-powered doghouse.

1. What would be the advantages of a solar-powered doghouse?

2. What would be the disadvantages?

3. Think of as many uses for solar energy as you can. Can you invent a use for power from the sun that no one else has considered?

4. What if we no longer had the sun as a source of light and energy? What might cause this to happen? Think of several ideas.

5. What would the effects be? Think of many types of effects—not just those related to energy.

SAFETY STANDARDS

In <u>Hit</u> <u>and</u> <u>Run</u> by Linda Atkinson (Franklin Watts, 1981), Susan accidentally hits someone and leaves the scene when she realizes that no one saw her do it. Traffic accidents are the most common cause of accidental death in America. Do some research on these statistics with the purpose of finding solutions to the problem.

1. What age person is most likely to be involved in a fatal traffic accident?

   _____

   Why do you think this is true? _____

2. During what months of the year are traffic fatalities most likely to occur?

   _____

   Why do you think this is true? _____

3. When was the speed limit standardized at 55 mph? _____

   Why was this done? _____

   What effect, if any, has it had on traffic fatalities? _____

   Do you believe the 55 mph speed limit is a good law? _____

   Why? _____

   _____

4. Do you wear a seat belt when you are in the car? _____

   Why? _____

   Do you believe seat belts save lives? _____

   Why? _____

5. What is the controversy over air bags? _____

   Why do advocates think they are better than seat belts? _____

   Do you believe they should be required in new cars? Give reasons for your answer.

   _____

   _____

6. What is MADD? _____

   What is the purpose of this group? _____

   _____

   Do you agree or disagree with their cause? Why? _____

   _____

7. Choose one factor in traffic accidents and think of as many ways to correct the problem as you can. Design some posters or make up a radio, television, or newspaper campaign to call public attention to the problem and your ideas for solutions.

THE POWER OF THE POST

1. Think of as many ways as you can that United States citizens can make their opinions known to government officials in Washington, D.C.

_____

_____

_____

_____

2. If the President of the United States were planning to do something that you opposed, how might you change his mind? Think of things you could do as an individual.

_____

_____

_____

_____

3. What would be the most effective way to organize a group to protest a Presidential decision?

_____

_____

_____

_____

4. Imagine that the Senate were considering a decision to require that all students go to school year around. Would you agree or disagree with such a decision? Give reasons for your answer.

_____

_____

_____

_____

_____

_____

_____

5. Research the name and mailing address of your Senator. Write a letter using the format on the next page.

U.S. GOVERNMENT

(Your address)

(date)

The Honorable (_____)
                        name
the address

Dear Mr. Senator:

(The first paragraph will tell why you are writing and what your opinion is.)

(Other paragraphs should tell what the reasons are for your opinion.)

(In the closing paragraph you should summarize your ideas, restate your opinion, and thank the Senator for considering your opinion.)

Sincerely,

(Your name)

Read <u>The Fragile Flag</u> by Jane Langton (Harper & Row, 1984). It is about a young girl who decides to enter a national essay contest about what the flag means to her and use the opportunity to let the President know she is against a weapon called the President's Peace Missle.

DELICIOUS DICTIONARY

In <u>The</u> <u>Search</u> <u>for</u> <u>Delicious</u> by Natalie Babbitt (Farrar, Straus, and Giroux, 1964), a civil war starts in a strange kingdom because of a disagreement over the definition of "Delicious." The Prime Minister said delicious was fresh fish, but others chose other foods. Some other examples from the Prime Minister's dictionary follow:

Affectionate is your dog.

Annoying is a loose boot in a muddy place.

Bulky is a big bag of boxes.

How would you define the following words?

Bewildered is _____

Careless is _____

Comfort is _____

Dainty is _____

Different is _____

Elegant is _____

Evil is _____

Fancy is _____

Forgetful is _____

Generous is _____

Gruesome is _____

Hasty is _____

Hoarse is _____

Ingenius is _____

Finish the alphabet on your own.

TORNADO WARNING!

1. Research what a tornado is and how it usually behaves. Indicate the ways in which the imaginary storm described below broke the rules. Mark out the incorrect or unusual information and pencil in the typical facts about tornadoes.

FREAK STORM

Four tornadoes hit a small town in Indiana on December 12, and ravaged the community for three hours. The funnel clouds were spotted north of town and moved southeast toward homes and businesses at seventy miles per hour. The first funnel cloud was estimated to be a mile in diameter with winds spinning clockwise at 250 miles per hour. The severe wind was accompanied by heavy rain and hail.

Could such a freak storm occur? Why or why not?

_____

_____

Read Night of the Twisters by Ivy Ruckman (Thomas Y. Crowell, 1984) for an account of the seven tornadoes that hit Grand Island, Nebraska, on June 4, 1980. See if these storms were typical or freaks.

2. What is the difference between a Tornado Watch and a Tornado Warning?

_____

_____

3. Where should you go for safety if a tornado occurs when you are:

    At home: _____

    Outside: _____

    At school: _____

    In a store: _____

    In a car: _____

Tornado Warning! (cont.)

4. How are tornadoes forecast? What improvements are being advanced?

_____

_____

5. <u>Night of the Twisters</u> by Ivy Ruckman (Thomas Y. Crowell, 1984) includes these descriptions of the storm that devastated Grand Island, Nebraska, on June 4, 1980:

>   "The roaring had started somewhere to the east, then came bearing down on us like a hundred freight trains."
>
>   "...the loudest noise I'd ever heard, whining worse than any jet."
>
>   "...the hail began. Once it got going, it hit us with the force of buckshot."

Write your own metaphors or similes. Make your comparisons as original as you can.

a. The sky _____

_____

b. The noise _____

_____

c. The wind _____

_____

d. The rain _____

_____

e. The hail _____

_____

f. The destruction after the storm _____

_____

6. Imagine your town is hit by a tornado. Your home and your family survive. Although there are no deaths or serious injuries, many homes and businesses are destroyed. What problems will you and your neighbors face <u>after</u> the storm?

EXTRATERRESTRIAL RIB-TICKLERS

In <u>The</u> <u>Computer</u> <u>Nut</u> by Betsy Byars (Viking Kestral, 1984), Kate meets a comedian from outer space. His jokes (starting on page 114) include:

    Q. What is green and goes ERRRRRRRRRRP?

    A. A Martian with indigestion.

    Q. How does a creature from the planet Rys tell time?

    A. With his Rys watch.

Think of several extraterrestrial terms and planets (real or imagined). Use these terms to change your favorite jokes to make them comedy material for an extraterrestrial creature.

Q. _____

A. _____

Q. _____

A. _____

Q. _____

A. _____

Q. _____

A. _____

Q. _____

A. _____

Extraterrestrial Rib-Ticklers (cont.)

Some of the jokes in <u>The</u> <u>Computer</u> <u>Nut</u> were based on assumptions about the creatures being joked about, like our elephant jokes. Here are some examples:

Q.   Is there something wrong with your throat?

A.   I have a Frogian in it.

*   (Frogians are small creatures from the planet Frogo)

Q.   How many Voykins does it take to wash a space shuttle?

A.   Two, one to hold the sponge and one to drive the shuttle back and forth.

*   (Voykins are not overly bright)

Create your own jokes of this type. Make up creatures to be the victims of the joke. Tell what characteristics of those creatures make the joke funny.

Q.   _____

A.   _____

*   _____

Q.   _____

A.   _____

*   _____

Q.   _____

A.   _____

*   _____

Q.   _____

A.   _____

*   _____

I AGREE/DISAGREE

The first Amendment guarantees Americans freedom of speech. Many people, however, have difficulty dealing with conflicting opinions. Some become so confused, they don't know what to believe. Others accept a viewpoint and cannot be swayed from it, regardless of factual evidence that their opinion is in error.

It is important to learn to evaluate opposing viewpoints in order to choose the most valid conclusion. It is equally important to be openminded regarding new information which might make it necessary to change your mind.

Agree or disagree with the following statements. Prepare arguments to support your opinion.

1. If the whole class agreed on a point of view, with the exception of one student, that lone student must be wrong.

2. In the example above, that student has no right to voice his opinion.

3. The best way to become well-informed on a subject is to examine all points of view regarding that subject.

4. It is possible for everyone to agree, and sometime later to find out all of them were wrong.

5. The news magazines and media news people are objective--not taking one side or the other.

As you read nonfiction accounts of controversial issues, you must determine if you are reading fact or opinion. Many fiction authors also write about subjects which many be open to opposing viewpoints. They will write a story about an imaginary event, presenting many factual items in the setting, but presenting their viewpoint in the fictional course of events.

Although you can enjoy the story regardless of your viewpoint, you will want to analyze your own opinions of the events while remembering the book is fiction.

WHO WON THE ARMS RACE?

Perhaps the only <u>facts</u> about nuclear weapons are that they kill, and both the United States and the Soviet Union have them. The statements below are <u>opinions</u>. Do you agree or disagree with them? State your reasons.

1. A nuclear war will send mankind back to the stone age.

2. The only way to secure peace is to be in a position of strength.

3. Currently, the Soviet Union has more military strength than the U.S.

4. No nation can win a nuclear war.

5. The lack of preparedness at Pearl Harbor should have taught us the need for military superiority.

6. The Soviet Union is the only nation which could possibly attack the U.S.

7. Stopping the buildup of military arms is essential for national security.

8. If the United States has more nuclear weapons than the Soviet Union, the world is safe.

9. Huge firestorms will follow a nuclear attack.

10. The smog and soot carried into high levels of the atmosphere after an attack will make the earth less affected by sunlight. It will be darker and colder.

11. Plants will not grow for years after a nuclear attack because of cold temperatures and lack of sunlight.

12. If we are armed for nuclear war, it is logical to expect it will eventually occur.

13. As far as twenty miles from the place a bomb hits, all people will be killed and most buildings would be destroyed.

14. Fallout shelters would be effective in a city hit by a nuclear bomb.

15. Survivors of a nuclear attack would be likely to die of starvation or diseases like plague, rabies, yellow fever, typhoid fever, or malaria.

Read <u>The Fragile Flag</u> by Jane Langton (Harper & Row, 1984)
<u>Wolf of Shadows</u> by Whitley Streiber (Knopf, 1985)

WORKSHEET REQUIRING THAT ALL ANSWERS CONSIST OF
EXACTLY TEN WORDS

John D. Jones enjoys irritating his mother and meeting difficult goals. Once he got an A on a science test on which he answered all questions with exactly ten words.

Rewrite these Newbery-Award winning titles so that they have ten words in the title without changing the meaning. Hyphenated words count as two words.

Example: <u>Roller Skates</u>: Ball-bearing wheels moving ankle-high boots across the floor

1. <u>Thimble Summer</u>: _____

2. <u>Rabbit Hill</u>: _____

3. <u>The Twenty-One Balloons</u>: _____

4. <u>Wheel on the School</u>: _____

5. <u>Island of the Blue Dolphins</u>: _____

6. <u>A Wrinkle in Time</u>: _____

7. <u>Shadow of a Bull</u>: _____

8. <u>Up a Road Slowly</u>: _____

9. <u>The High King</u>: _____

10. <u>Summer of the Swans</u>: _____

Read <u>The Animal, The Vegetable, and John D. Jones</u> by Betsy Byars
(Delacorte, 1982)